Ike Turner – King of Rhythm

IKE TURNER

KING OF RHYTHM

By

John Collis

First Published in Great Britain in 2003 by
The Do-Not Press Limited
16 The Woodlands
London SE13 6TY
www.thedonotpress.com
email: ike@thedonotpress.com

ISBN 1 904 316 24 7

British Library Cataloguing in Publication Data. A
catalogue record for this book is available from the
British Library.

1 3 5 7 9 10 8 6 4 2

Printed and bound in Great Britain

This book is dedicated to St Louis musician
and broadcaster Roy St John

IKE TURNER

KING OF RHYTHM

Table of contents

Acknowledgments

I am most grateful to Fred Rothwell, author of *Long Distance Information: Chuck Berry's Recorded Legacy*, for his comprehensive discography of Ike Turner's record releases. Roger St Pierre lent me a wheelbarrow-load of vinyl, Cliff White and Rob Hughes were helpful with printed material while Ian McLagan, formerly of The Faces, reminisced about his meeting with Turner. Roy St John in St Louis gave me one or two useful leads, and finally thanks to Jim Driver of The Do-Not Press, who commissioned this book over a pint in The Dog and Bell.

John Collis, August 2003

Introduction

Rock 'n' roll was not born, springing fully formed from the womb of some magical recording studio, one day down South. But we are tempted to take an arbitrary starting point in telling its story. We always have an urge to push thumbtacks into history, to stop it wriggling.

The most logical departure date, perhaps, is 1955. In that year three black artists – Chuck Berry, Fats Domino and Little Richard – began to make their first waves in the pop charts, the white charts. The only blacks to invade the hit parade previously had been close-harmony crooners like the Orioles, but now the world was readier for something raunchier. Above all, these three made the crossover without compromising their sound.

No doubt Berry's light vocal tone was useful when he served up his first motorvatin' masterpiece, 'Maybellene', helping to gain airplay across the board. After all, he had sometimes been known as 'the black hillbilly' during his apprenticeship at the Cosmopolitan Club in St Louis. But Fats Domino, with 'Ain't That a Shame', remained as he always had been, and always would – a New Orleans barrelhouse easy-rider – and Little Richard's 'Tutti Frutti' remains one of the wildest, *blackest* records of all time.

Within a year Elvis Presley had broken out of the South with 'Heartbreak Hotel' and, as Sherlock Holmes often remarked, the game was afoot. Yes, logic guides us to 1955 as the time that rock 'n' roll became clearly identifiable as a musical phenomenon, and it is therefore a convenient starting point for the story.

The problem is that such an account could well airbrush Ike Turner out of that story entirely. He must be getting used to it – widen the scope beyond the limitations of rock 'n' roll and he is often still, it seems, a non-person, even before his reputation for marital violence became well-known. I have in front of me a book published in 1969 with the ambitious sub-title *The Story of Black Music*. Ike Turner is not mentioned! This is a little like publishing *British Politics Since 1939* with no references to Winston Churchill.

What is the reason for this? The most convincing answer is that by 1955 he had already sparked the revolution, that bridge between ghetto music and the commercial pop charts, and then he had moved onwards – and not necessarily upwards. At least, not yet. If rock 'n' roll burst out with Little Richard's demonic 'Awopbopalula-awopbamboom', an inspired perversion of his sacred singing style, then its story requires what in the movie industry is now called a prequel. And the star of the prequel is Ike Turner.

Little Richard himself confirms this. In the foreword to Turner's ghosted autobiography *Takin' Back my Name* he says: 'When people talk about rock 'n' roll they talk about Chuck Berry. They talk about Fats Domino. They talk about Little Richard. They leave the main thing out… we came on later. Before all these people, Ike Turner was doing his thing. He is the innovator.'

At the start of that *annus mirabilis* 1955 Turner was 23 years old. As a child in the early 1940s he had played piano in Clarksdale, in the Mississippi Delta, for such visiting legends as 'the second' Sonny Boy Williamson and local guitar hero Robert Nighthawk, a reincarnation of Robert Johnson. Turner was a teenaged, schoolboy bandleader and, when he was nineteen, his band travelled to Sam Phillips's Memphis Recording Service studio and cut a car-loving boogie called 'Rocket 88', long pre-dating Berry's fascination with the subject.

Many people, including Sun owner Sam Phillips, have been tempted to call this the first rock 'n' roll record, even though they know there is no such thing. And if there was, it might be Hank Williams's MGM debut 'Move It On Over', from 1947. Or 'The Fat Man', Domino's 1949 recording. Or 1946's 'Guitar Boogie' by Arthur Smith. Or Big Joe Turner's 1953 hit, 'Honey Hush'. In fact, someone could set up a 'first rock 'n' roll record' Internet chat room to while away the long drinking hours.

Turner was not limited to his explosive piano technique. He played proto-rock guitar behind BB King, Howlin' Wolf and many others. He became a youthful talent scout and record producer, dangerously sending Wolf tracks from Sun, as Sam Phillips soon renamed his Memphis studio, both to the Bihari brothers in Los Angeles and Leonard Chess in Chicago, which pleased neither. He tried his hand at country music, mirroring Berry's youthful leanings, and was cumbersomely credited as Icky Renrut.

By 1956 Turner was playing band residencies in St Louis, Berry's town, since he had long outgrown Clarksdale. While the rock 'n' roll flame leapt into life all around him his CV proved that he had already rocked around the block several times. Few noticed. In St Louis he was in a home-town triumvirate with Berry and Albert King, but the world still hadn't heard of him – after all, even 'Rocket 88' had been credited to his saxophone player Jackie Brenston.

And so the main reason for this book is to attempt to put the record straight. Turner is best known, if he is known at all, as Mr Tina, domineering, drug-crazed (he has estimated that he spent $11million on cocaine, but how would he know?) and violent. He was all of those things, at least at times, and this is perhaps a second reason for the tut-tutting airbrush of history.

Turner's story is inevitably 'top heavy'. It was as a prodigious youth that he displayed his genius in all aspects of the southern music business, and so this period is dwelt upon, as well as his tempestuous time with Tina. On the other hand, the fifteen years from the mid-70s up to his jail sentence in 1990 for cocaine possession can be summed in the single word 'cocaine', and so are dealt with more summarily.

In 2001, when in his 70th year, Turner released a new studio album, *Here and Now*, including an exuberant revisit, fifty years on, to 'Rocket 88'. It was a defiant comeback statement that confirmed his credentials as one of the great figures of blues, R&B and rock 'n' roll. Whatever he may have got up to in his private life, as a musician he deserves a testimonial as one of the great Kings of Rhythm.

Down on the Delta

Before King Cotton arrived the Mississippi Delta was a dense, sweaty, tropical forest. A jungle of huge trees draped with vast hanging curtains of vines, humid and impenetrable. Spared the threat of all but the most persistent Choctaw Indian hunters, wolves, bears and big cats lazily fended off swarms of insects, snoozing beside alligator creeks, edging around black swamps. It was a primeval world.

The Delta is part of the alluvial plain of the mighty river that marks its western border, and with each flood across the centuries more thick, black mud was laid down over the putrid compost of dead plants, building up the richest, deepest soil in the world. The word 'Mississippi' means 'great water' in a number of local native American dialects.

An extraordinary variety of thick-trunked, cathedral-high trees thrust upwards, with scrubby plants spreading out below to choke the ground. Almost half the area of the United States is within the drainage basin of the Mississippi/Missouri, rinsing its mud down to the Delta. The river was discovered by Hernando De Soto in 1541, and its valley was claimed for the French in 1682.

In 1817 Mississippi joined the Union, and by the middle of the century the draining and clearing of the land had begun – land too rich to avoid the attentions first of the loggers and then the planters. The State developed an agricultural, one-crop economy, and by the early 20th century 80 million acres of jungle had been cleared to make way for cotton. The landscape is now flat, black and endlessly dreary, fading into infinity, and Highway 61 drones through it, barely swerving an inch from its ruler-straight course in the stretch south of Memphis down to Clarksdale.

Mississippi was traditionally one of the keenest supporters of slavery, and in defence of the indefensible it seceded from the Union in 1861. The South at this stage was still overwhelmingly agrarian – no town in Mississippi, neighbouring Arkansas, North Carolina, Florida or even Texas could boast as many as 10,000 inhabitants. Mississippi suffered hugely as a result of the Civil War but was readmitted to the Union in 1870. When control of the State fell into the hands of the pro-slavery 'Redeemers' in 1875 a one-party system was set up and deliberate efforts were made to disenfranchise blacks. These initially took the form of simple intimidation – for instance the open wearing of guns on election days – but in 1890 a more formal scheme became part of the State's laws whereby all adults had to be able to read, comprehend and summarise the US Constitution.

This enabled registration officials to discriminate in favour of illiterate whites, by deeming that their understanding was sufficient, while debarring uneducated blacks from the vote. It was not until 1962 that the first black student, James Meredith, enrolled at the State University, and it took until that decade before the pro-white provisions in state law were completely dismantled. It was in this atmosphere first of slavery, then of subjection to white plantation owners, against a backdrop of State law that deliberately discriminated against blacks, that the blues evolved.

A fertile breeding ground for both cotton and the blues, the Delta runs south from, as tradition has it, 'the lobby of the Peabody Hotel' in Memphis down to Vicksburg. With the Mississippi River defining its western edge, it is confined in the east by the Coldwater River, which then joins the Tallahachie, which in turn becomes the Yazoo. In area it spreads in a lozenge shape for some 13,000 square miles, a quarter of the State's total, and it is bolstered by huge levees to protect the crops from flooding.

Clarksdale, in Coahoma County towards the north of the Delta, was first settled in 1848 and became the regional centre for cotton trading. The plantations were ranged around it, funnelling their produce through Clarksdale to the outside world, including the textile mills of Lancashire. In recent decades the farmers of the region have diversified in response to a number of factors – the destructive boll weevil, mechanised cotton picking and the flight of blacks to the industrial north among them – but Clarksdale remains the trading focus for the newer crops, soybeans, peanuts, rice and corn, as well as cotton.

Clarksdale proudly claims to be the home of the blues, and the long list of musicians who were either born there, born nearby or based in town for a significant time includes 'the father of the blues' W C Handy, John Lee Hooker, Muddy Waters, Robert Johnson, Elmore James, Gus Cannon, Arthur Crudup, Son House, Charley Patton, Howlin' Wolf, the second Sonny Boy Williamson and Bessie Smith.

The Delta Blues Museum has recently been established in Clarksdale in a large brick building that dates back to the years of the First World War. It was at first the depot for the Yazoo and Mississippi River Valley Railroad, later becoming the freight depot for the Illinois Central. Among Clarksdale's celebrated sons honoured here is Ike Turner.

The Young Ike

Ike Wister Turner, nicknamed Sonny, was born in Clarksdale on 5th November 1931, to Izear Luster Turner and Beatrice Cushenberry, who already had a ten-year-old daughter, Lee Ethel. They were creoles, of mixed black and French descent. Izear preached at the local Centennial Baptist Church and 'Momma B' was a seamstress. The house at 304 Washington was a wooden 'shotgun' shack, so called because the three rooms – living room, bedroom and kitchen – were built in the cheapest format, one behind the other, and so with the doors open a shot could be fired through the front door and out at the back.

Clarksdale was of course a segregated town in

those days, with blacks living on the east side of the railroad. But cotton kept it lively, with a thriving blues scene. Racism also thrived, and Turner's father was a tragic victim of it. It may be that he was having an affair with a woman who was also involved with a local white man, a vicious redneck.

Whatever, a gang kicked their way into the house one day, blindfolded Izear and drove off with him. After torturing him for hours they dumped him, barely alive, back in the yard. He had been so badly kicked that his abdomen wall had been ruptured and his guts exposed.

There was no black hospital in Clarksdale, and the white one refused to admit Izear or even treat him. Eventually the health department erected a tent in the Turners' yard as a makeshift ward. In those days a black invalid either got better naturally or died, and it took Izear two or three years to die of his wounds. Ike was five or six at the time. By 2001, it should be noted, his version was that his father had been shot, but the details of torture in *Takin' Back My Name* seem convincing. The tent, presumably, had been provided to prevent turning the tiny house into a hospital ward.

Later, when he was about fifteen, Ike witnessed another chilling example of the way racial tension erupted into hatred and violence. A black man armed with a gun went crazy, and in his frenzy he shot dead over twenty white men. The Ku Klux Klan arrived and captured him. They cut his throat, cut off his penis and placed it in his throat.

As a child, Ike was often left to fend for himself while his mother worked. Sometimes he helped in that work, learning how to cord the edges of sofa covers, but he also led a blind man around town, collected and sold junk, raised chickens and even begged at the bus station, pretending to be deaf and dumb. So by the age of seven he was an expert hustler, ingenious in inventing new ways to make a few cents.

Years later he talked about this to Cilla Huggins of *Juke Blues*. 'I would buy the chickens – little bitty – and I would pay $15 for a hundred... Out of a hundred you save maybe 65 or 70 of them that would live... And then I would raise them till they get to be pullets, and then I would sell 'em to the stores and things.' He also made use of the scraps of material his mother had finished with, making rag rugs and selling them.

Beatrice soon married again but Ike's stepfather, Philip Reese, didn't take to his adopted son. After one row Ike crept up behind him and knocked him out with a piece of wood. Terrified, Ike cycled all the way to Memphis, although for a lot of the way he was clinging to the backboard of a fast-moving truck.

Ike lived on the streets for days until a man who worked in one of the hotels took pity on him and got him a job cleaning the lobby. But soon he felt homesick and, gambling that his mother's relief at seeing him back safely would protect him against his stepfather's anger, he returned to Clarksdale. He was right. In the late 1950s, when Ike was a club star in St Louis, his mother died and he moved his stepfather into a house there, so there was eventually a reconciliation of sorts.

Ike had a particular childhood friend, Ernest Lane, who was indirectly responsible for Ike taking an interest in music. Ernest's father had a piano, and played a bit of ragtime, but to Ike this was barely more exciting than the music he had heard in his father's church. However, one day as they walked towards Ernest's house on Yazoo Street they heard loud boogie-woogie flooding from the window.

It was Pinetop Perkins, who played with

Sonny Boy Williamson on the flour-sponsored
King Biscuit Time on KFFA. Perkins was born
down in Belzoni but from the late 1930s was
based in Clarksdale, working on the plantations during lean times but now a local star. 'He
was whooping the piano to death, man,' Turner
recalls. 'It excited me more than anything in the
world.'

And so his first piano lessons came courtesy
of one of the greats of boogie-woogie, and it is
the spirit of Pinetop Perkins that crashes out of
'Rocket 88'. Also at this time, the mother of
schoolfriend Raymond Hill, later saxophonist
with the Kings of Rhythm, owned a café where
people like Perkins and Robert Nighthawk
played, and the young Ike learned by hanging
out.

Momma B saw in her son's newfound enthusiasm for something other than hustling and
mischief an opportunity for some gentle black-
mail – settle down to your lessons and you can
have a piano. So he worked just hard enough to
earn one, but the teacher his mother sent him to
was too formal for his tastes and, after learning
a few rudiments, he would spend his piano-
lesson dollar in the pool hall. But in the
meantime he was picking up tricks from

Pinetop, and learning by imitation. 'My mother she was thinking I was learning all this boogie woogie and stuff from the lessons,' he told Cilla Huggins.

He continued his career as a juvenile hustler, and at the age of ten was dealing in moonshine whiskey. About that time the house caught fire and the piano was badly burned. The ingenuity that enabled a child to distil and peddle booze also allowed him to restore the piano using felt, rubber, off-cut wood and glue, and he then learned how to re-tune it – another handy trade.

The next step in his musical career came when he took an after-school job as lift-attendant at the Alcazar Hotel. A radio station, WROX, operated from the second floor, and on his meal breaks Ike would watch disc jockey John Friscilla at work. It wasn't long before he was recruited to run errands and then to cue up the records.

'I'd run up to the second floor and look through the window at the guy spinning records,' Turner told writer Margaret Moser in 2001. 'He saw me and told me to come in and showed me how to "hold a record". I'd sit there and hold it until the one playing stopped, then I'd turn a knob and the one I was holding would play. Next thing I know, he was going across the street for coffee and leaving me in there alone. I was only eight [a bit older, I would suggest]. That was the beginning of my thing with music.'

Turner was so keen and precise that the station manager then offered him the late-afternoon shift as disc jockey. This gave him access to all the new releases arriving on the desk and, since these were the days before the centrally-devised playlist, Ike had a free hand. He mixed the obvious, like Louis Jordan, with the surprising – hillbilly. 'My favourite music is country,' claims the one-time Icky Renrut, straight-faced.

Ike got serious about music when he enrolled in high school. There was a traditional school band at Myrtle Hall, but he could not play a brass instrument and so was debarred. With like-minded enthusiasts he joined a huge local rhythm ensemble in town called The Tophatters. They played big-band arrangements, sight-reading. Since Ike had always played by ear he learned from the records at home and then pretended to be reading the music during rehearsals. The band played dances in and around Clarksdale.

Before that, however, came a revelatory

moment for the twelve-year-old, new to senior school. News had got around that he could play piano, and he was called up to perform during assembly, in front of the whole school. He was terrified, rattled off a few bars learned from Pinetop, and retreated. Even though it increased his standing with the girls (and at that age he was already sexually active) he realised that he was not a natural front man, too shy to hog the spotlight.

This reticence has stayed with him. In his most celebrated manifestation, in the Ike and Tina Turner Revue, he was everything *but* the star – organiser, employer, businessman, writer, arranger, guitarist, producer – but usually a background figure on stage, even doubly so – at the back *and* with his back to the audience.

After a few months there was a rift within The Tophatters. Those who wanted to continue playing the dance-band jazz of Tommy Dorsey and Harry James renamed themselves The Dukes of Swing, while those attracted to R&B – like Turner and his friend Clayton Love – were reborn as the Kings of Rhythm. Turner was the natural leader, 'a genius' in Love's opinion. 'We wanted to play blues, boogie-woogie and Roy Brown, Jimmy Liggins, Roy Milton… ' Turner recalls. At the outset, then, it is clear that their first ambitions were simply as a 'covers' band, a living jukebox. The rivalry between the two factions spinning off from The Tophatters even led them to stage an open-air 'battle of the bands' from two flatbed trucks every other weekend.

The Kings of Rhythm honed their repertoire with a weekly Wednesday residency at Clarksdale's Harlem Theater before getting bookings throughout the Delta and beyond. Turner also sang in an *a cappella* group and then he and his friend Ernest teamed up with Robert Nighthawk. Turner left his mother's house and moved into the Riverside Hotel, where Nighthawk stayed. He and Ernest began by acting as unofficial roadies for Nighthawk, before joining him on piano and drums.

This suited Nighthawk, because on some gigs he would be expected to play for twelve hours at a stretch, from early evening until the last customers left way after dawn. On radio he was scheduled to compete against Sonny Boy Williamson and Pinetop Perkins, and could not pull in as many listeners, so he had less clout when it came to negotiating working conditions. But with a trio that included two lead instruments it was always possible for one of the musicians to leave the bandstand occasionally for a drink, to relieve himself or even to enjoy a round-the-back quickie with one of the girls from the bar. With Nighthawk scoring more gigs than the Kings of Rhythm could at this early stage, this was a solid apprenticeship for the teenaged Turner.

'We played juke joints,' he told Margaret Moser. 'We'd start playing at 8.00pm and wouldn't get off till 8.00am. No intermissions, no breaks. If you had to go to the restroom, well, that's how I learned to play drums and guitar! When one had to go, someone had to take his place.'

Before the Sunrise

In October 1949 Sam Phillips, a 26-year-old disc jockey and music promoter at the Peabody Hotel, took a lease at $150 a month on 706 Union Avenue, Memphis, formerly a radiator repair workshop and, bit by bit, he began to install recording equipment. By January 1950 he was open for business, as the Memphis Recording Service. In the early days he would accept any work to keep the business afloat, for example by providing sound souvenirs of local weddings and by transferring private tape recordings to disc.

But Phillips had a clear idea of what he really wanted to do. As he told Sun Records historian Martin Hawkins in 1984, his intention was to record 'singers and musicians from Memphis and the locality who I felt had something that people should be able to hear. I'm talking here about blues, both the country style and the rhythm style, and also about spirituals or gospel music and about white country music.' Earlier he had put his ambitions more simply and directly: 'The Negroes had no place to record in the South... So I set up a studio in 1950 just to make records of those great Negro artists.'

In May he secured a deal with 4 Star Records in Los Angeles to provide masters of local artists. The first that they picked up on was a blind blues singer and pianist, Lost John Hunter, with 'Cool Down Mama'. This deal soon faltered, but Phillips signed another one with Jules and Saul Bihari, owners of the Modern and RPM labels. Modern had been formed in Los Angeles in 1945 and soon established that key to success, a nationwide network of distributors. The deal with the Memphis Recording Service was signed in 1950, and Phillips was also planning his own label, Phillips, in partnership with the unrelated disc jockey Dewey Phillips. Their first release was 'Boogie in the Park' by one-man-band Joe

Hill Louis, originally sent to Modern but recalled when the idea of the home-grown label took shape.

The Louis recording was an important step forward for Phillips, not least because Louis was a local radio star and was able to confirm to other artists that the studio owner treated him fairly. In November, though, disappointed by sales of what proved to be the only release on his own-name label, Phillips secured a deal for Louis with Modern, who had a slicker distribution system in place. He was also sending them masters by local disc-jockey and blues guitarist BB King, Walter Horton and Rosco Gordon. At the beginning of 1951, however, after a year in business, he was still waiting for his big breakthrough record. Soon, however, he made a useful contact with the recently-formed Chess label in Chicago, who had enjoyed early success with Clarksdale émigré Muddy Waters.

In March Turner and the Kings of Rhythm were driving between gigs when they dropped in on a BB King club date in Chambers, Mississippi. Turner knew King from a time when the blues guitarist had appeared in Clarksdale, and he claimed that he had persuaded King to let his band sit-in and play a number. They went down so well that the club owner booked them for a weekend residency. King, meanwhile, recommended them to Phillips in Memphis.

The problem was of course that Turner's band played covers of current jukebox hits, and didn't have any material of their own, so a degree of bluff was necessary. Phillips wasn't going to buy a cover version – after all, he had recorded some of the originals. It was during the actual drive to the Memphis Recording Service that saxophone-player-turned-singer Jackie Brenston came up with the idea for 'Rocket 88', about a recently-launched Oldsmobile motor, the Rocket Hydro-Matic 88. Based loosely on an existing car song, Jimmy Liggins's 1947 Specialty single 'Cadillac Boogie', it was to prove hugely influential in its turn – Little Richard has admitted that he stole Turner's manic piano intro for 'Good Golly Miss Molly', and indeed the lineage is unmistakeable.

The band arrived at the studio before the song was finished, and Turner worked out an arrangement on the spot. Brenston later admitted his debt to Liggins. 'They're both basically the same. The words are just changed.'

'Rocket 88' combined expert jump-boogie ensemble playing by the teenage band with a valve-popping Phillips production. Willie Kizart's enthusiastic guitar was over-amplified to the point of thrilling, unheard-of distortion, an effect assisted by the fact that his amplifier had fallen off the roof of the car on the trip up Highway 61, and so was damaged. The resulting electronic rattle comfortably predates the time in 1958 that Link Wray stabbed a pencil into the cone of his amp before recording his crude, one-trick, reverberating masterpiece 'Rumble'.

Turner meanwhile hammered the piano keys into submission as if this was a do-or-die chance to be noticed, which it may well have seemed at the time, and Raymond Hill's saxophone was deliciously vulgar, far more Illinois Jacquet than Ben Webster. And young saxophonist Jackie Brenston was drafted in to give his creation a muscular, urgent vocal reading.

Maybe every element of this thrilling record had some traceable ancestry, with the possible exception of amplifier abuse, but the overall package did seem to offer something new and exciting. The session was completed briskly with a routine blues, 'Come Back Where You Belong'.

Phillips sent the masters off to the Chess brothers, once Brenston's mother had signed a contract on behalf of her teenage son. There were intended to be three elements involved in the artist credit – singer and nominal writer Brenston, bandleader and arranger Turner, and the Kings of Rhythm. Wires seemed to get crossed, and Chess pressed up a disc credited to 'Jackie Brenston and his Delta Cats'. Turner and the rest of the band received session fees of $20, and Phillips later bought out Brenston's interest in the song for a curiously precise $910. Of course this rankled with Turner – he waited a long time before getting some sort of comeback when he insisted on receiving an artist credit for 'River Deep, Mountain High', the writing, recording and production of which he played no part in. But by then he had a powerful bargaining chip in Tina.

Sam Phillips's friend and erstwhile partner Dewey Phillips was a disc jockey on the local – white – radio station WHBQ, presenting a show called *Red, Hot and Blue*. He played 'Rocket 88' to death, while the Chess brothers worked on their own contacts. The song hit number 4 in *Billboard*'s Rhythm & Blues chart in May 1951 and within a month reached the top, staying in the chart all summer. In Philadelphia, local disc jockey and leader of hillbilly band The Saddlemen, Bill Haley, heard the record and changed the direction of his career, developing with his own 'Rocket 88' a sprightly pastiche of black rhythm & blues that culminated in the anthem 'Rock Around the Clock' – another cover version.

'"Rocket 88" was the record that really kicked it off for me as far as broadening the base of the music and opening up wider markets [was concerned],' said Phillips. Its success came in the nick of time, enabling him in June 1951 to resign from all his other broadcasting and promotional commitments, the cumulative strain of which was driving him towards a breakdown, to concentrate on his studio.

According to Phillips, he had to insist on Brenston being the singer. 'I said, "Ike, man, you can't sing [but] Jackie here has this vocal that we can really go somewhere with".' But no sooner had the band found success – however much Turner's ego might have been hurt – than they began to fragment. Their usual singer Johnny O'Neal signed a solo contract with King Records, where he was teamed with the

Tiny Bradshaw combo. Raymond Hill nursed band-leading ambitions, and was annoyed at seeing no real return from the record. And Jackie Brenston saw himself as a star, so some of the band decided to try their luck with him.

Amid this chaos Chess Records started shouting for a follow-up record to capitalise on the success of 'Rocket 88'. As Phillips saw it, Turner had 'taken Jackie's band away from us,' though Turner had little control over events. A desperate situation called for desperate measures, and so Phillips called in an unreliable, alcoholic singer in his late 30s, but one who on his day could match Brenston's exuberance – Billy Love. His recording of 'Juiced', credited to Brenston, was sent off to Chicago as the successor to 'Rocket 88'. Phillips bought out Love's interest in a one-off payment in order to keep Brenston's flag flying. As writer, pianist and singer Love received $100. The irony is that this is a wonderful record, a worthy, booting sequel to the hit, with Love maintaining a ferocious energy. However, it had nothing to do with the so-called 'Jackie Brenston and his Delta Cats'.

Brenston's own follow-up came next, 'My Real Gone Rocket'. Perhaps its close similarity to the hit limited sales, because it did little.

Brenston continued to record for Chess until 1953's 'Starvation', with diminishing sales returns. 'I was a greenhorn,' said Brenston. 'I had a hit record and no sense.' He joined Lowell Fulson's band as sax player for a couple of years – steady work, since the pioneer electric bluesman was one of the top circuit attractions of the day. Fulson's Chess debut, 'Reconsider Baby', is one of the classics of the decade, and was later covered by Elvis Presley. Then Brenston returned to the Kings of Rhythm.

However, Turner still harboured a grudge about Brenston's star billing on what remained the band's only hit. In spite of Brenston's great jump-blues voice he was given few opportunities to sing, and Turner frequently fined him for his drinking, along with partner-in-crime Raymond Hill. Jimmy Thomas, who joined the band in 1958 as the main vocalist, told *Blues Unlimited* in 1980 that Brenston and Hill 'was drinking that really bad shit... that stuff they used to drink you probably wouldn't allow it in your house. Not even to wash the floor!'

When Ike and Tina had their first hit in 1960, 'A Fool in Love' on the Sue label, the company also cut a Brenston single, 'Trouble Up the Road' and 'You Ain't the One'. Brenston left Turner's band for the last time in 1962. His next collaborator, Sid Wallace, recalls: 'The only thing he was basically concerned about then was a bottle of wine.'

Brenston recorded once more in 1963, with Earl Hooker in Chicago, cutting 'Want You to Rock Me' and 'Down in my Heart'. He then returned to Clarksdale and lived in alcoholic obscurity until he died in 1979.

The Kings of Rhythm would soon reappear after Brenston left, with some of the other defectors also returning to the fold, but in the meantime Turner had to look for other work. On one of his trips to Memphis – commuting by bike as he had done when he ran away from home as a child – he walked in on a BB King session. The song was 'You Know I Love You'. Joe Bihari, co-owner of Modern/RPM, was having trouble getting the sound he heard in his head, and identified the possible problem as the jazz inclinations of pianist Phineas Newborn. On a break, Turner sat down at the piano and started playing. 'That's what I want!' was Bihari's reaction.

BB King was well aware of Turner by this time. He recalled that visit to Clarksdale, referred to earlier, when the precocious Turner introduced himself – the introduction that in turn put Turner in touch with Sam Phillips. 'A young guy, around fourteen-years old, came to this theatre where we were gonna play. This was Ike Turner… and young as Ike was he was a really fine piano player. He came and heard us rehearsing and he said, "My God, you guys need help." So he got up and played with us that night.' Years later, King was to call Turner 'the best bandleader I've ever seen'. The King version, that Turner alone sat in on the earlier gig, sounds more convincing than Turner's claim that King allowed the whole band to set up and perform.

So Turner played with King again on that struggling session. A grateful Bihari paid him a fee of $30 – a 50% increase on his return from the half-million-selling 'Rocket 88' – and while 'You Know I Love You' remained in the can for a while Turner went on to play on King's first hit 'Three O'Clock Blues'. The earlier song then charted as the follow-up.

In the meantime Bihari immediately saw Turner as a conduit to the musical talent of the Delta and beyond. 'So I took him down to Clarksdale, Greenville, Batesville, Marks… just a few places,' says Turner. To his talents as pianist, guitarist and bandleader Turner was about to add talent scout, producer and writer, with the Bihari brothers in Los Angeles and the Chess brothers in Chicago competing for his services.

Bihari started paying Turner $100 a week plus generous expenses, which often more than doubled his salary. 'The top job for anybody,' reflected Turner, 'was something like $45 a week... I had more money than anybody [in town].'

Bihari's approach was to give Turner a Buick and send him out trawling the South for talent. Turner would arrive in town, go to the bar or barber's shop, and ask for names. He'd audition, note down the details, and promise to be back. Then, every six weeks or so, Joe Bihari would drive across from California with a portable, four-input Magnecord recorder, pick up Turner and go hunting for hits.

Down into Louisiana, across into Arkansas and Georgia, they recorded an unparalleled wealth of local talent. When it came to cutting a full-size band, they'd be cramming all the instruments through the four channels. And as they travelled they'd also be glad-handing local dealers, distributors and disc jockeys, promoting the fruits of previous trips.

In addition Turner had the job of writing original material for the artists he tracked down, unaware that in return for paying him a handsome retainer the Biharis were registering the copyright on his songs. He reckons that he 'wrote 78 hit records for the Biharis', but at the time he was delighted with the cash in hand.

Since the late 1940s Modern, and then its offshoot RPM, had been carving a niche in blues history. In Detroit in 1948 Clarksdale migrant John Lee Hooker cut his hypnotic debut 'Boogie Chillen', backed by 'Sally Mae', which was eventually a million seller, and over the next three years he gave Modern hits with 'Hobo Blues', 'Crawling King Snake Blues' and one of his lasting classics, 'I'm in the Mood'.

From 1951 onwards BB King delivered fifteen successive hits to RPM. Modern also cut the young Bobby Bland, brought to the label by Turner and billed as 'Robert', before his fruitful move to the Duke label. They had the Howlin' Wolf sides sent to them by Turner, and RPM released an early Turner disc, backed by the Ben Burton Orchestra, 'You're Driving Me Insane'.

During one of Turner's brief marital partnerships RPM was also home to 'Looking for a Baby' by Bonnie and Ike Turner, and the label released the huge Rosco Gordon hits 'Booted' (where Turner's double-dealing meant a release for the disc on Chess as well) and 'No More Doggin'".

Scouting for Talent

Turner's first great success had already made his name by this time: BB King. After three years in Memphis, busking and working with Johnny Ace, Bobby Bland and Earl Forrest as the Beale Streeters, he landed a ten-minute spot on radio station WDIA in 1948. As with Sonny Boy Williamson and Robert Nighthawk, King found that radio exposure was not only employment in itself, but a calling card that led to more and better-paid live work.

King broadcast at 3.30pm every day, sponsored by a patent medicine called Peptikon. This was not just the indigestion remedy its name implies, but according to King it 'was supposed to

be good for whatever ails you, like toothache.'
In common with all WDIA presenters, King
was required to improvise the sponsor's
message. 'Peptikon sure is good, you can get it
anywhere in your neighbourhood.' Years later
he recalled, 'that was the beginning of BB King'.
His first records, released on the Nashville label
Bullet, were cut at the radio studio, but he then
moved to the Biharis' RPM, who were using the
Memphis Recording Service.

Station WDIA was crucial not only to BB
King's career – it brought about a broadcasting
revolution that spread throughout the US.
Founded on 7 June 1947 by two white
Memphis entrepreneurs, John Pepper and Bert
Ferguson, it failed to make commercial
headway in competition with the city's five
existing stations, all chasing the white con-
sumer's dollar. WDIA tried ballads, country
and western, even an afternoon symphony.

Then, suddenly realising that 47% of the
Memphis population was black, Ferguson
thought the unthinkable, 'programming for the
Negro people'. It had never been done before. A
leading member of the black community,
history teacher Nat Williams, was hired to host
a 4.00pm show after school was out. The

station agonised over what to call his show –
the words 'black', 'coloured' and 'Negro'
seemed inappropriate. In a segregated, often
bitterly divided city the black area was referred
to by many whites as 'nigger town'. WDIA sani-
tised this racialism and came up with 'Tan
Town Jamboree'.

Williams was so nervous that he found
himself laughing on air, out of sheer fright, but
it became his warming trademark. Programme
director Chris Spindell, a white woman (long
after all the presenters were black, the adminis-
trative staff and management remained white),
recalls that on the morning after the launch on
25th October 1948 she arrived for work half
expecting to find a burning cross in the station
yard.

News of the show spread by word of mouth
and its audience built swiftly. Shopkeepers
learned that the black man's dollar was worth
just as much as the white man's. WDIA spread
black programming across the schedule – blues,
gospel, women's domestic issues – and soon
Williams was presenting a daily show before
school as well as after it.

And so in December BB King arrived in
Memphis from Indianola, Mississippi, walking

for miles in the pouring rain clutching his guitar to his chest, and he arrived at WDIA 'shy, scared and wringing wet', according to Spindell. But as soon as he stood in front of an audition microphone his charisma was apparent.

Rufus Thomas joined WDIA in 1950 and, with frequent diversions to walk the dog and do the funky chicken, he stayed there for the rest of his life. 'We's feeling gay tho' we ain't got a dollar, Rufus is here so let's hoot and holler.' The young Elvis Presley was captivated by the station, and learned to sing black. To those in the local music business like Ike Turner, Sam Phillips and the Bihari brothers, WDIA was the passport to their audience. Before long there were nearly 500 radio stations across America offering black programming. Meanwhile, Presley was creeping into black clubs and, so legend has it, was hiding behind Turner's piano.

Having secured his roving ambassador job with the Biharis thanks to a BB King session, Turner repaid the favour later in 1951, when he was still only 19. Using the fuller acoustics of the local YMCA rather than Phillips's studio, Turner produced 'Three O'Clock Blues' for King, a huge R&B success in December. This enabled King to sever his tie with WDIA, which of course had limited his scope as far as getting to evening gigs was concerned, for a life on the road that has lasted ever since. Like Bob Dylan, BB King's later career has been a constant tour. 'What else am I meant to do?' he once asked me. 'I don't like golf.'

While Turner's dealings with King were above-board, he found himself juggling loyalties when it came to Howlin' Wolf, the other great success of his early A&R/production career. The mighty Wolf, whose bone-jarring, passionate voice was one of the greatest in the blues, came to full-time music late – he was 42 when the Chess brothers persuaded him to move to Chicago in 1952.

But he was already a legend in the Delta before the war, and so was a living link with the pioneers like Robert Johnson, Charley Patton and Son House. After army service he settled in Arkansas as a farmer, driving a tractor during the week, performing at weekends. From 1948 he was also working for KWEM in West Memphis as disc jockey and performer, and seemed content with a balance of farming and music.

At around the same time that Turner was

cutting 'Three O'Clock Blues' with King he brought the Wolf into Phillips's studio to cut the powerful and atmospheric coupling of 'How Many More Years' and 'Moanin' at Midnight'. The urgency of the Wolf's vocals was perfectly complemented by the attack of his guitarist Willie Johnson and, when leased to Chess, it hit the charts in November 1951. But at the time Turner, who was effectively working as a house producer for Sam Phillips and dealing with the Chess brothers, was under his $100-a-week contract with the Biharis.

St Louis saxophonist Oliver Sain, incidentally, recalls a later confrontation between Turner and Howlin' Wolf when, in frustration at the great man's obtuseness, the featherweight Turner punched the mighty Wolf. Perhaps fortunately for the subsequent development of black music as well as Turner's health, the Wolf looked at first perplexed and then vaguely amused, but couldn't be bothered to raise a paw in retaliation.

There was no satisfactory resolution of the conflict of loyalties as far as competing record companies were concerned, certainly not in the way that Turner dealt with it – he re-recorded the Wolf, across the State border in West

Memphis and with Phillips safely out of earshot, using the same material and some new songs. He sent the results to Modern/RPM, and so at times the Wolf had versions of a song appearing simultaneously on rival labels.

Far from learning to avoid duplicity, Turner tried to do a similar double deal with Elmore James, who was under exclusive contract to Lillian McMurray of Trumpet Records in Jackson, Mississippi, due east of Vicksburg. When he and Bihari encountered James in Canton, up the road from Jackson, they signed and recorded him. Trumpet sued and Modern shelved the record. But James, ironically, decided in favour of the Biharis, sat out his Trumpet contract for a year, and signed with Modern. So maybe the dodgy dealing paid off in the end. Turner played piano on many of James's subsequent Modern sides, regional successes that failed to make the national chart.

As mentioned earlier, Rosco Gordon was a further artist who became involved in a tug-of-war between Modern/RPM and Chess, suggesting that Sam Phillips and Turner could not resist playing this particular game. It seems unlikely that they ever felt they could play off the two labels against each other, 'auctioning'

masters to the highest bidder. More credible is
the thought that, in an uncertain and volatile
market, they believed they had the apparent
security of two clients. But it was a tactic that
brought too many problems.

Gordon was another erstwhile Beale
Streeter, an engaging and highly distinctive
artist. The skipping beat and stabbing syncopa-
tion of his finest sides were clearly one of the
inspirations for the Jamaican music that developed later in the decade. Phillips first cut him in
February 1951 and sold 'Rosco's Boogie' to
Modern/RPM, who were impressed enough to
issue two further singles later in the year.

Then Gordon cut his first masterpiece,
'Booted' – with a rollicking sax solo by that
rhythm king Raymond Hill – and instead of
posting it west to Los Angeles Phillips sent it to
the Chess brothers. The Biharis slapped down a
writ and recovered the rights, which resulted in
the record reaching number 1 thanks to cumulative sales on two labels. In February 1952 the
dispute was settled – the Biharis got Rosco
Gordon, the Chess brothers got Howlin' Wolf.

It is indicative of the fact that this double-
dealing was by and large seen simply as part of
the cut and thrust of the record business,

usually to be resolved by a sternly-worded lawyer's letter, that when the Duke label was set up in Memphis a year later Phillips sold *them* a Rosco Gordon master, provoking more legal huffing and puffing from the Biharis. Then, in 1952, the Biharis set up a new label, Meteor, and a recording studio in Memphis. Phillips, the middle man, saw the writing on the wall and was prompted to found his own label, Sun.

With Ike Turner on piano and Joe Bihari as producer, Elmore James recorded some stunning sides for Meteor. Particularly effective were tracks like 'Hawaiian Boogie', cut live in Club Bizarre in Canton, Mississippi. Among the artists found during their field trips was Boyd Gilmore, who cut 'All In My Dreams' for Modern. But the guitarist wasn't up to scratch so Bihari simply dubbed on James's guitar track from his 'Please Find My Baby'.

He recorded later James sides at Universal in Chicago, the studio favoured by Chess Records before they installed their in-house equipment. Turner played piano on such 1954 Chicago cuts as 'Quarter Past Nine', 'Where Can My Baby Be' and 'Sho' Nuff I Do', often with Raymond Hill on saxophone.

In the meantime Phillips had granted Turner

his own studio session in August 1953. His band now consisted of himself on guitar, his new wife Bonnie on piano, James Wheeler and Thomas Reed on saxophones, plus regular drummer Willie Sims. Ten tracks were cut, with Turner singing on six and Bonnie on the others. Maybe, given his opinion of Turner's singing, Phillips was just trying to keep his valuable A&R man happy – he didn't release a single result of a long day's work.

Two of the cuts, 'I Told My Girl About You' and 'Camping in Canaan's Island', remain in the can to this day – a 2001 release on Varese Sarabande titled *Ike Turner – The Sun Sessions* gave a detailed picture of this period in Turner's career but left these two alone. The others first came to light on the Charly label in the late 1970s, on Volume 3 of their valuable vinyl series *Sun – The Roots of Rock*, subtitled 'Delta Rhythm Kings'.

Although Bonnie shows a nimble boogie-woogie piano style on 'Love is a Gamble' her voice is weak – on this track, on 'Old Brother Jack' (set to a greasy blues riff as lazy as the 'Little Red Rooster') and a silly two-tempo novelty 'Way Down in the Congo'.

The limitations of Turner's voice are also

apparent, though far worse singers have made a living, and he brings a pleasantly roughened tone to 'Get It Over Baby', with a melody that looks forward to Ray Charles's 'Hallelujah I Love Her So'. On the slow blues 'How Long Will It Last' the outstanding feature is his guitar work, with the distinctive tremolo effect that he christened the 'whammy bar'.

Turner evoked New Orleans for the mid-tempo, sax-led 'You Can't Be the One for Me', while the ballad 'Why Should I Keep Trying' has a close-harmony gospel feel. Given Turner's good fortune and skill in finding strong vocalists for the Kings of Rhythm, Phillips's reluctance to feature him as vocalist is understandable. However, there was one surprise in this session, and it may well have been the last track to be recorded.

'I'm Gonna Forget About You' is a sprightly, guitar-led jump blues, and captures that same proto-rock feel as 'Rocket 88'. It is further proof that Turner was way ahead of his time – five years later up-tempo numbers like this were being recorded throughout the States, and they were called rock 'n' roll.

The doubts about Turner's voice – Bonnie's even more so – were confirmed when on-off

Kings of Rhythm singer Johnny O'Neal fronted the band for the sexist, 'Rocket 88'-styled 'Ugly Woman' and the slow 'Dead Letter Blues', adorned with a busy Turner guitar part. Surprisingly, though, these also remained on the shelf – maybe Phillips and for that matter Bihari felt that the world was not ready for a song about an ugly woman, even though O'Neal confirms his undying affection for her. The paths of Turner and O'Neal would cross again in St Louis, where the latter had an outfit called The Hound Dogs.

A further session around this time, which produced an RPM single 'Love is Scarce' and 'The Way You Used to Treat Me', also featured Turner's vocals, though he was billed on the label as Lover Boy. Dennis Binder, replacing Bonnie on piano, was the singer on another track cut at this session, 'I Miss You So'. A further session produced a release on the Crown label with the portentous title 'Hey Miss Tina'.

Queens and Kings

And so in 1953, aged 21, Turner was married to Bonnie, singer and pianist and also a Turner, although later he would claim not to remember if he actually married her or not. This particular manifestation of amnesia was to become commonplace – Turner's most recent (and divorced) wife Jeanette may or may not have been his thirteenth. Bonnie was a former girlfriend of Raymond Hill. This was Turner's third marriage, if indeed marriage it was. When he was in his mid-teens he married Edna Dean Stewart, who came from Ruleville, and they lived with his mother. Although Ruleville is only 36 miles from Clarksdale Edna got homesick and went back there for good. It could be that Turner is still married to her and has been a serial bigamist ever since – although when his relationship with Tina Turner broke down he was quick to claim that they had never been legally married anyway.

Turner stayed in Yazoo City for a while, playing in a local club and living with Thelma Dishman, though it seems they did not marry. The second Mrs Turner, apparently, was Rosa Lee Sane, in West Memphis but, in spite of her name, she was soon confined to an asylum.

Bonnie, however, was an accomplished performer in the Ruth Brown mould, and inspired Turner to put the Kings of Rhythm back together. With his wife on piano Turner switched to guitar. Saxophonist Hill returned to the fold, augmented by another ex-Tophatter, Eugene Fox, and Bobby Fields. Turner taught his nephew Jesse Knight the rudiments of playing bass guitar, and Bob Prindell replaced Willie Sims, the original drummer.

Tipped off by Clarksdale blues guitarist Earl Hooker about gigging opportunities in Florida, the band headed out there. But Turner's marriage to Bonnie proved as short-lived as his previous experiences. She started having an affair, left Turner in Sarasota, and moved to New York.

Without Bonnie the remaining members of the band stayed together after the brief Florida experiment, though with Willie Sims returning on drums, and gigs in and around Clarksdale built up steadily. They were part of a growing local scene, with other former Kings of Rhythm like Jackie Brenston and Clayton Love also active, and so Turner and Joe Bihari decided to set up a studio in the town rather than always having to commute to Memphis.

Turner was soon married again, but his motive this time guaranteed that it was as doomed as its predecessors. He started fooling with a woman called Alice, but she was also going with the former Kings of Rhythm singer Johnny O'Neal. Turner asked her to marry him with the idea of cutting out O'Neal.

The studio, too, was fated. On their field trips recording for Modern/RPM, the white Bihari and the black Turner had often run into trouble simply for travelling together. Now, a black and a white were partners in a business located on the white side of the railway tracks, employing black musicians. Racists soon tore the place apart.

No doubt to console himself, Turner got married yet again. The teenaged Anna Mae Wilson from Greenville was another pianist, and she joined a new Kings of Rhythm line-up in 1956. Hill, Brenston and Knight were on board, with Eddie Jones now playing tenor sax and Eugene Washington on drums. Turner's sister Lee Ethel had moved north to St Louis, the first big city up the river from Memphis, and he began to think that maybe the future of the band lay there.

He got the Kings of Rhythm a gig at a club in the rough East St Louis district across the river. The booking was extended and led to a growing date sheet in the area – soon they secured a residency at Club Manhattan. So began a golden period for the Kings of Rhythm.

King of St Louis

In the middle-late 1950s, in the years before the future Tina Turner sang her way into the band, the Kings of Rhythm became the biggest attraction in St Louis, working constantly. At this time St Louis boy Chuck Berry moved from local celebrity to the peak of his popularity as the biggest black star of the era, a hero whenever he returned home – which was frequently, as St Louis has always been his base. The great bluesman Albert King was also active in the city, and his group was often augmented by Berry's pianist Johnnie Johnson, particularly once Berry realised that he could make more money without a band.

This triumvirate of stellar residents competed

for audiences with a constant flow of visiting musicians, who either included the major city of the region in their itinerary or stopped off there for a while, typically on the familiar blues migration from the Delta to Chicago. The founding father of Chicago blues, Muddy Waters, had been one such transient in the mid-40s, working in the munitions factory and moving on in peacetime, when the factory closed down.

St Louis is sometimes described as the South's northernmost outpost, and a music scene constantly enriched by southerners must have been fundamental to creating this image – a tough, ugly, northern industrial town rocking to the rhythms of Mississippi and Louisiana. And it still had a heart in those days, a stroll from club to club, before the flight to the suburbs fragmented the musical scene and abandoned the middle of the city to freeways and cars.

For Turner and the Kings of Rhythm it all began at a club run by a man named Ned Love, who soon gave them the security of a four-night weekend residency. They then added Mondays at the 2151 Club on St Louis Avenue, and before long, according to Turner, 'we were doing fourteen jobs a week'.

Then came Club Manhattan, situated like Love's club in East St Louis, at 1320 Broadway. The band helped turn the bare brick building into a music venue, and it became their home. The white promoter George Edick had them play at his Club Imperial on West Florisson Street in St Louis proper, where he also booked Chuck Berry, and this helped them crossover to the young white audience in town. Edick also featured the band on a television show, *Party Time at the Club Imperial*.

He was impressed by the discipline that Turner imposed on the band. Suits and ties, no drinking when working, punctuality, sacking for backsliders. Now that he was appealing to both blacks and whites Turner felt in a position to insist on no colour bar either way in any place he played. He would adapt the set, with more downhome blues over in East St Louis, but the businessman in him told him to keep faith with all the band's followers.

The popularity of the Kings of Rhythm brought with it problems, particularly since they attracted women both when they were on and off the stage. Jealousy led to fights, and fights in East St Louis meant guns. The sax player Eddie Jones was once called outside

Club Manhattan by someone looking for trouble, and a wild-west gun battle left them both injured. Turner claims that he persuaded the authorities to provide the band with deputy sheriff badges, thus entitling them to carry guns legally. This does seem somewhat far-fetched, that young, black, R&B musicians should be officially handed a licence to kill. Particularly as it didn't seem to prevent them from being busted regularly in the aftermath of Jones's shoot-out.

Turner maintained his connection with Joe Bihari in Los Angeles, and in the years 1954 and 1955 the band travelled out there to cut singles with the Kings' featured vocalist Billy Gayles, and also with Johnny Wright and Richard Berry, who a year later formed the Pharaohs and cut his garage classic 'Louie Louie'. The collaboration with Turner was the lively 'Rockin' Man'. Berry was recording at the time for a new Bihari imprint, Flair, and the Kings also had a couple of singles released on the label, Latino-flavoured instrumentals that did little commercially.

In 1956, with Gayles still fronting the band, the Kings of Rhythm began visiting Cincinnati to record for local label Federal. These sessions show the pre-Tina band at their absolute peak, a tantalising hint of what could be taken for granted in the St Louis clubs of the day. Gayles had an expressive voice with an appealing touch of hoarseness and surprising range, at home with a slow, contemplative blues like 'Let's Call It A Day' as with the up-tempo numbers that formed the bulk of their repertoire, booted along by the rasping saxophones of Hill and Jones (and often Brenston as well).

The most impressive result of the first Federal session, on 12th March 1956, was 'I'm Tore Up', launched by Turner with a guitar introduction that Freddy King would have been proud of, and pumped along by Jesse Knight's insistent bass line. The lyric is concerned with that familiar blues problem, spending the Friday pay check at the bar on the way home, and it struck enough chords to become a regional R&B hit. Throughout these sessions, Turner shows a touch on blues guitar that effortlessly puts him on a par with the greats.

The sound was fattened by Jackie Brenston's baritone sax for a second visit on 12th September, with Turner using treble-heavy distortion on his guitar on three up-tempo rockers, notably 'Just One More Time'. In contrast,

Gayles sounds convincingly like Lloyd Price on a slow, New Orleans groove called 'No Coming Back'.

On the following day Brenston was to the fore, sometimes with a touch of Little Richard in his voice, and the New Orleans feel was retained for such pleading songs as 'The Mistreater'. The vocal styles of Gayles and Brenston were satisfyingly distinctive, stressing the revue nature of the entertainment that Turner had developed.

The band visited Cincinnati for a third time in November 1956 to back the doo-wop vocals of The Gardenias, while in April 1957 another impressive voice, that of on-off member since schooldays Clayton Love, cut four sides, at a session completed by two instrumentals. There's a touch of The Coasters on 'She Made My Blood Run Cold', although the lyric lacks the incisive wit of Jerry Leiber. Particularly impressive is the jump blues 'Do You Mean It', introduced by a crisp, high-register Turner guitar solo.

In the years before Tina transformed the nature of the Revue, these Federal sessions are a fine reminder of the tight, disciplined rocking that made the Kings of Rhythm stars of St

Louis. None of the sides, however, translated their appeal into the national R&B list. Perhaps the best shot at guessing the mood of the charts is the rasping instrumental 'Rock-a-Bucket', from the 1957 session, with Hill doing his finest Earl Bostic impersonation in front of a solidly riffing band. This just predates the chart success of 'Raunchy' by Bill Justis, a similar idea, but 'Rock-a-Bucket' was not greased on to sufficient radio stations for it to take off nationally.

Turner's latest marriage, and he'd lost count by this time, broke up when Annie Mae started having a fairly public affair with a local policeman. Turner couldn't complain – he had never bothered to conceal his own never-ending sequence of relationships. Fred Sample replaced Annie Mae in the band, but for a while she continued as their manager.

Turner bought a house in Virginia Place, East St Louis, with enough room for the whole band to party all night long, every night. The violent jealousy of cuckolded husbands and boyfriends increased, guns were loosed off at the house, and Turner claims that in one revenge attack a roadie was castrated, and bled to death.

He further boasts that he briefly employed a

guitar player called Jimmy, but had to fire him
because he kept getting uncontrollable feed-
back and distortion. When Turner next heard
of him, of course, he was called Jimi Hendrix.
In fact, though, and this is confirmed by
Hendrix, his brief stint with Turner came
during the mid-1960s (the heyday of the Ike
and Tina Revue), in between jobs with Little
Richard and The Isley Brothers, and just before
he was discovered by Chas Chandler.

Enter Tina

'Tina was my Little Richard,' Turner says. Praise indeed, since Richard is the artist he admires most. But it took him a while to appreciate her extraordinary vocal talent.

In 1957 Annie Mae Bullock began turning up at Kings of Rhythm gigs at Club Manhattan. At this time her older sister Alline was going out with the drummer, Eugene Washington, and 'Little Ann' came along too, sometimes with a group of friends including her classmate Pat. Because she was only sixteen Eugene had her sit where he could keep an eye on her. He was the first to notice that she would always sing along with the numbers.

Turner was not interested in Little Ann. She was too skinny, and he preferred her friend Pat. Although Ann was desperate to be invited on to the bandstand to sing, Turner kept putting her off. Then one night, while the musicians were outside on a break, Turner remained up on stage playing the organ. He tended to stay safely away from the audience during the interval as it was likely to include several women he was sleeping with at the time, and he was anxious to avoid scenes and cat-fights on the dance floor. Bad for business.

Ann recognised the song he was doodling with as BB King's 'You Know I Love You', the 1952 follow-up hit to 'Three O'Clock Blues', both of them produced by Turner. Washington came back into the room at that point and, hearing her singing to herself, brought over a microphone. As soon as she began to sing, Turner was convinced. As the rest of the band drifted back he ran through the numbers she knew, and thus she joined the Kings of Rhythm.

Not immediately, however. Her mother was furious when she found out that Ann had sung with the band – Ike Turner already had a reputation around St Louis for loose and temperamental behaviour – and she put a stop to Ann's adventure. Later in the same summer, though, Turner needed a singer urgently, and he came over to Ann's house on his best Sunday-tea behaviour to try and charm her mother.

It worked, and Ann joined the Revue for a probationary college gig in Columbus, Missouri. She came to no harm, Turner made sure of that, and so her mother agreed that she could sing with the band at weekends but not on school nights. Although Ann was only featured for a part of the show – she remembers it being three songs – her raw, emotional and uninhibited style of singing brought a new dimension to the band. 'Her voice was different for the type of music we were doing,' said Eugene Washington. 'Things just exploded right from there.'

Ann soon started going with the sax player Raymond Hill, and by November 1957 she was pregnant. Turner, meanwhile, was with another girl from the crowd, Lorraine Taylor. Ann liked Hill because he only had two or three women on the go at a time, 'where everybody else had six or eight or ten'. After each gig the band and their entourage would go back to Turner's house, party all night and sleep all day.

Hill, however, soon abandoned Ann, left St

Louis and returned to Clarksdale, having badly broken his ankle in a fight. And as Ann's pregnancy became obvious, Lorraine suspected that Turner was the father. In a jealous rage one night she stole Turner's gun, threatened Ann, locked herself in the bathroom and tried to commit suicide. The bullet passed through her chest but somehow she survived.

Life in the house was getting a little too lively for an expectant, single mother still at high school. Ann went back to live in her mother's house, left school in summer 1958 and on 20th August Raymond Craig was born. On 3rd October Lorraine – in spite of the trauma of the shooting – also gave birth, to Ike Junior.

Soon Ann was juggling motherhood, a day job as a nursing assistant at Barnes Hospital and what had by now become a regular nightly stint with the band. She moved out, finding a flat near her mother, but as her commitment to the band increased – as did the wages Turner paid her, to $25 a week – she found it convenient to take the chance and move back into Turner's house.

It seems that 'Little Ann' first recorded with the band in Chicago, in 1958. 'Box Top' appeared on the Cobra label, a backroom operation that nevertheless sported such artists as Magic Sam, Otis Rush and Buddy Guy. Willie Dixon, the central fixer in the Chicago blues scene, is best known for his association with Chess Records as producer, writer and session bass player, but he was under no secure contract and would often work for rivals like Cobra and its sister label Artistic.

Turner plays supporting guitar on such Rush hits as 'All Your Love' and 'Double Trouble', and Guy recalls that Turner and his band were on his second Artistic single 'This Is The End'. Surprisingly, given Dixon's local standing, he says that 'Ike was a little above Willie Dixon on that session, and he's the one that put the sound together for the record.'

Ann's second session was in the following year, at Technisonic in St Louis, and the discographical details suggest that the pattern was becoming set for the touring revue of the following decade. Ike had by now dubbed her Tina Turner and there were three backing vocalists, Dolores Johnson, Joshie Armstead and Eloise Faye, billed as The Ikettes. The two tracks, 'That's All I Need' and 'My Love', were leased to the Sue label, the home for all subsequent Ike and Tina product until late in 1963.

Though the revue format was in place, the record was credited to Ike Turner and the Kings of Rhythm.

For the real breakthrough, however, the band had to wait until 1960, when they went back to the studio in St Louis, and in Tina's recollection (and, it must be admitted, other contemporary recollections) this was in fact her first record with the group. By now a singer named Art Lassiter was working with the Kings of Rhythm, but he also sang numbers by Ray Charles under his own name, backed by a female trio dubbed The Artettes (Charles's girls were The Raelettes). And so Ike's group followed the style and were called the Ikettes.

He had written a song for Lassiter to cut at the session, 'A Fool in Love'. Come the day of the recording, however, The Artettes turned up but Lassiter stayed at home, having argued with Turner about the financial arrangement for the day. And so The Artettes – Frances Hodges, Robbie Montgomery and Sandra Harding – became Ikettes and Tina was given the song to sing, as a guide track for Lassiter if and when the dispute with Turner was resolved.

Sue Records was based in New York and was run by a black entrepreneur, Juggy Murray.

Although Motown was now up and running in Detroit black-owned labels were still unusual. Murray had in fact set up his label just before Berry Gordy, in 1958. He 'didn't know [Turner] from a hole in the wall' when first contacted by him, but in 'A Fool in Love' he heard a hit. He travelled down to St Louis and was amazed to discover how popular Turner was – no hit record, no real reputation outside his home town, but king of St Louis.

Murray insisted that it was Tina's vocals that made the record, was not interested in Lassiter re-cutting it, and offered a huge $25,000 advance. He seems to suggest that this was the first Turner release on Sue, though the earlier 'That's All I Need' St Louis session has a prior Sue catalogue number.

Now on the brink of national success, Turner's private life was even more complex than usual. Having had a second son, Michael, by Lorraine in 1959 he had also got Ann/Tina pregnant, padding the corridor between the two. He was then charged with a mysterious financial crime that he describes as 'interstate transportation of forged cheques and conspiracy.'

He now needed money in a hurry to hire lawyers, and Murray insisted on having a follow-up to 'A Fool in Love' in the can before he'd advance more cash. But Tina was not only pregnant, she was in hospital with jaundice. She smuggled herself out and the tracks 'I Idolize You' and 'Letter from Tina', already written and arranged, were cut overnight.

'A Fool In Love' was credited to Ike and Tina Turner, and in August 1960 it reached the second spot on the R&B chart. More significantly in terms of sales it made number 27 on the pop listing. With the Kings of Rhythm now re-christened the Ike and Tina Turner Revue, they set off on a four-month nationwide tour to capitalise on the record's success.

Tina wasn't properly fit, and she was now very pregnant, but Turner gave her no choice. Their first date under the new name was in Cincinnati, Ohio. Life on the road was to become the norm – record success was sporadic, but there was always live work to be had. Meanwhile the jury failed to agree on a verdict when Turner came to trial on the financial charge, but on a retrial he was found not guilty.

If the 1956/57 Federal sessions showed the pre-Tina Kings of Rhythm at their exuberant peak, then 'A Fool in Love' was dramatic confirmation of how Turner transformed the band by putting Tina up front and adding The Ikettes to the show. The last link with the high-school jump-blues band had been broken, and the 1960s revue was born. From the moment Tina starts wailing a gospel-like introduction of remarkable intensity, it is impossible to imagine the song without her, or to see this as a demo version for Lassiter to inherit. Like all the great wailers – Ray Charles, James Brown, Linda Jones among them – she never mistakes shouting for emotional expression. Other singers – all the way from Whitney, Nebraska to Houston, Texas – have been unable to make this distinction, but the young Tina Turner, even at her most frenzied, always conveyed convincing feeling, raw and bleeding.

In 1960 and into the new decade, between rock 'n' roll and the blues revival, New Orleans records were charting regularly – Fats Domino of course, Lloyd Price, Jessie Hill, Lee Dorsey, Ernie K-Doe *et al*. Crescent City music helped to keep rockers sane when too many cleancut crooners were being flooded on to the market. Turner somehow anticipated the trend – though recorded in St Louis and released in New York, 'A Fool in Love' strikes a chunky, New Orleans groove cunningly in keeping with the times.

With the record climbing the late summer charts and peaking in October, the Revue played the legendary Apollo Theater in Harlem, on a mouth-watering bill including Hank Ballard and the Midnighters and, suitably, a trio of New Orleans talent – Joe Jones (charting with 'You Talk Too Much'), Lee Dorsey and Ernie K-Doe.

On the Road

Throughout his life, most of Turner's problems have been self-inflicted, caused by serial infidelity, brash spending, hot-tempered arguments with fellow musicians, his drug habit, and an arrogant assumption that he could wriggle out of anything. With Tina's confinement approaching he began training a lookalike, who joined the tour and was to take over when the baby was born, to keep the show on the road. It turned out, however, that not only was the phoney Tina a prostitute, but that she was leading her clients to believe that she was the real Tina. Turner claims to have been unaware of his new protegee's sideline, though it perhaps seems unlikely that he wouldn't have worked it out for himself and taken advantage of a 100% discount. Just another problem, then.

Tina went into labour unexpectedly early when the caravan reached Los Angeles, and Turner had to fly back to St Louis for his retrial. On 27 October 1960 Tina gave birth to Ronald Renelle, but when one of The Ikettes visited her she learned about the other 'Tina'. She discharged herself, found the strength to beat up the impostor – to survive life with Ike Turner, she often had to discover previously unsuspected physical and mental reserves – and went back on stage two days after Ronald was born.

Lorraine decided that she'd had enough of looking after one of Turner's two families back in St Louis, and threatened to abandon her children by him if he didn't assume responsibility. He and Tina now had care of four children: Lorraine's sons, Ike Jr and Michael; Tina's son by Hill, Raymond Craig; and baby Ronald. They were put in the charge of various childminders while the Revue travelled on.

Turner made a couple of decisions at this stage aimed at guaranteeing work and full houses, though they were also the cause of the relentless schedule. He kept his price low, sometimes as little as $300, and he played small clubs, even ones with just 100 capacity. Gigs like the Apollo, he reasoned, could not be relied on every week, and a full house was good publicity. When Dire Straits first went to America on the back of a huge album success, their manager Ed Bicknell adopted a similar strategy – they could have played vast stadiums but the venues may have been half-full, so he opted for standing-room-only clubs, with hundreds of disappointed punters on the pavement every night. A little unfair on latecomers, but good for publicity.

This was the Ike and Tina pattern, night in and night out, for much of the 1960s – the most successful black road revue of the decade was usually playing in dives. James Brown and BB King, those other indefatigable travellers, often played to far bigger houses, but Turner remained cautious. He stayed out on the road 51 weeks of the year, with a short break in January before starting all over again. The working year started in Los Angeles, fanning out through California for three months. They then headed south and east, into Arizona, New Mexico and Texas before travelling through the Deep South. This led them to the eastern seaboard, up towards New York, inland to the industrial cities beside the Great Lakes, through the mid-west to the Rocky Mountains and then back towards Los Angeles for the autumn. It was a relentless schedule.

Turner's work load must partly be due to the fact that, in spite of the number of white buyers for 'A Fool in Love', the Revue never really 'crossed over' as a live act. It seemingly didn't occur to Turner to go for the college and festival crowd, who were opening up a new world of opportunity for artists like Muddy Waters and John Lee Hooker. However, it is perhaps equally likely that young white promoters who could deal comfortably with a lone, grateful bluesman balked at hiring the demanding Turner and his intimidating entourage.

Turner insisted that everyone created precisely the Ike and Tina sound he heard in his head. He certainly had that in common with James Brown, with his reputation for imposing a fine for one bum note, a sacking for two. For the first half of the 1960s the most faithful Ikettes were Robbie Montgomery and Jessie Smith from St Louis, and Venetta Fields from New York. Not necessarily, however, at the same time. Musicians and back-up singers, the latter also expected to rehearse the dance routines that made a vital, sexy part of the overall spectacle, inevitably came and went. The constant touring, Turner's volatile character, low pay and zero security took their toll.

'It was constant hard work,' recalls Tina. On arrival in a new town Turner would seek out the local recording studio to work during the day, and after the gig he'd be sketching out arrangements on his guitar in the back of the car. This is the time when, according to Tina, the violence began. 'It was torture, plain and simple.' Turner would beat her and humiliate her in a totally unpredictable manner, his mood suddenly darkening, his fists flying. What Tina cannot explain, beyond vague terms of masochistic dependency, is why she put up with it for so long.

A successful follow-up to 'A Fool In Love' proved elusive. The coupling of 'I Idolize You' and 'Letter from Tina' was rushed out but only had enough momentum to break into the lower reaches of the charts, followed by 'I'm Jealous' and 'You're My Baby'. However, it was not until the following year, 1961, that a New York session really did the trick.

Playing guitars on the date were Mickey

Baker and Sylvia Vanderpool, and it is Mickey rather than Turner who duets with Tina on the wonderful, preachy 'It's Gonna Work Out Fine'. As Mickey and Sylvia, the duo had first charted in 1957 with the hypnotic 'Love Is Strange', which along with a lesser but equally attractive hit 'Dearest' was one of the numerous black records covered by the young Buddy Holly in his west Texas garage. Later in 1961 they were to have further success with 'Baby You're So Fine', but in the meantime they added just the touch of magic to 'It's Gonna Work Out Fine' that Turner needed to break back into the charts in a big way.

Apart from Ike and Tina, the only survivors from the 'A Fool in Love' session were bass-player Jesse Knight and drummer 'TNT' Tribble. The Ikettes were now Eloise Faye and Joshie Armstead, and the current male singer with the Revue, Jimmy Thomas, augmented their wailing back-up vocals. A smash on the R&B charts, more importantly the record went to number 14 on the *Billboard* Hot Hundred, with 'Won't You Forgive' on the flip. Thomas was arguably the most accomplished of all the male singers to pass through the ranks. In 1966, reviewing a Royal Albert Hall appearance by the Revue, Bill Millar noted in *Soul Music* that Thomas was 'as exciting and polished as many a more well-known soul artist'.

With diminishing chart returns, three singles from the 'I Idolize You' session kept the Ike and Tina flag flying modestly in the Hot Hundred until the summer of 1962. 'Poor Fool', teamed with 'You Can't Blame Me', reached number 38, 'Tra La La La La' and 'Puppy Love' number 50 and 'You Shoulda Treated Me Right' with 'Sleepless' number 89.

'Poor Fool' was 'A Fool in Love' revisited, and Turner couldn't win the trick the second time around. 'Tra La La La La' was lightweight but 'You Shoulda Treated Me Right' deserved better – a solid R&B belter with saxophones to the fore, while the menacing slow blues 'Sleepless' made for a great double-sider.

However, Turner did have one substantial hit during this period. With erstwhile Ikette Dolores Johnson taking the lead vocal, swapping places with Tina, the novelty number 'I'm Blue' was leased to the Atco label – credited to The Ikettes to avoid contractual problems with Sue – and soared to number 19 early in 1962.

Turner then delivered an instrumental album to Sue, the highlight of which is his virtuoso blues workout 'Prancing'. This swaggering display of genius had been his theme tune in the old days. Once again his dexterity, control of tone and dynamics, and sheer inventive energy show Turner to be the equal of the elite blues guitarists, and in particular he evokes the attacking style of Freddie King.

There were two further albums on Sue, with Tina restored to the microphone, but Turner's long – by his standards – deal with the label ended in 1963 when the final Sue single 'Worried is a Hurtin' Inside' failed to make the chart. Indeed, the commercially barren period persisted until late in 1964, but meanwhile the Revue were out there every night on the road.

The success of 'It's Gonna Work Out Fine' meant that Turner had money flowing into his bank account, and in 1962 he left St Louis and bought a house in Los Angeles. He was to return to Missouri in the future, but his mind was now set on life in LA. As local disc-jockey Gabriel has noted: 'St Louis got too small for Ike. He went to California twice and came back again, but the third time he went and never came back again.'

Before Turner left St Louis a new Ikette joined the Revue, the only white girl ever to shake a tail feather alongside Tina. Bonnie

O'Farrell wasn't with them long – down South a white face in a black band was particularly dangerous – but her brand of blue-eyed soul was soon to be hugely successful with husband Delaney Bramlett as Delaney and Bonnie, who had their first hit in 1970 with 'Comin' Home', featuring Eric Clapton.

Bonnie got her chance in a hurry, when Turner fired one of the band and lost the musician's girlfriend, an Ikette, as well. Bonnie was experienced locally, performing with such St Louis stars as Albert King and Little Milton Campbell, but travelling with the Revue was a new and sometimes frightening experience. In Kentucky she tried to disguise her skin colour with fake tan, which in those days gave a somewhat unconvincing orange hue to the complexion.

When a gang of white youths taunted her as the band travelled down the freeway, and Turner lured them to follow him into a narrow side-turning before pulling a gun on them, she decided it was time to leave.

At around this time Ike and Tina got married, sort of. Turner insisted that it was a sham, an impromptu joke. After they had moved into the Los Angeles house some of the band took a brief break from the road down in Tijuana, Mexico. Having visited the strip clubs and sex cabarets that formed the town's main attractions they were all sitting in a restaurant booth when the house photographer offered to take their picture. He then suggested that he marry them for a tiny fee, and simply pronounced them man and wife. But Turner now insists that he has only been legally married once, that all the other liaisons were casual, and that he was not yet divorced at the time of the Tijuana jaunt.

Tina remembers it slightly differently – Turner suggested marriage, drove the two of them to Tijuana and found a grubby back-street lawyer to witness a document – but she accepts that they certainly didn't have a wedding, and that it didn't feel like a marriage. As far as the Revue was concerned it made no difference, since on stage she was already Tina Turner.

As Juggy Murray tells it in *I, Tina*, $40,000 of Turner's newly healthy cash-flow was the advance on a renewed contract with the Sue label, which Turner promptly spent on a ranch-style bungalow in southern Los Angeles and then failed to honour, sending Murray third-rate, unuseable material to keep him quiet.

However, Ike and Tina product did begin to surface on other labels, so if Turner had indeed agreed to a renewal of the Sue contract surely Murray would have sued. Early in 1964 'If I Can't Be the First' and 'I'm Going Back Home' appeared on Sonja, which also released 'You Can't Miss Nothing That You Never Had' and 'God Gave Me You'. There were two 1964 releases on Innis, the double-sided 'Here's Your Heart' and then 'You Can't Have Your Cake (and Eat It Too)' with an instrumental b-side, 'The Drag'.

And then in October of that year Ike and Tina returned to the Hot Hundred, admittedly only for a heady three weeks peaking at number 95, with 'I Can't Believe What You Say' backed by 'My Baby Now', and they were now on Kent.

This was the start of a baffling process of label-hopping that was to continue for the life of the Revue. At the heart of it was Turner the control freak. He would create the product and then he trawled around for the best deal. Next time the deal might be different, because he was always available for auction.

Label Hopping

The Kent deal revived Turner's relationship with the Bihari brothers, who owned the label. Although 'I Can't Believe What You Say' was Ike and Tina's last Hot Hundred hit before 'River Deep, Mountain High' in 1966, the Bihari recordings are a strong reflection of the Revue at the time. Other tracks from this period were released on the Biharis' long-standing Modern label. Some, like 'He's the One' and 'Something's Come Over You', were reworked attempts to repeat the magic of 'A Fool in Love' and 'It's Gonna Work Out Fine', but there are some gems among them.

The fast-moving 'I Can't Believe What You

Say' certainly deserved better, as did the marvellous 'Goodbye, So Long', one of the most energetic recordings that Tina, now at the height of her powers, ever cut, with her vocals urged along by Turner's ivory-busting, finger-bleeding piano part. Although this 1965 release performed respectably in the R&B chart, peaking at number 32, it just failed to break into the Hot Hundred, while the follow-up 'I Don't Need' only reached number 134.

The quality of Turner's recorded work at this time, and the on-the-road popularity of the Revue night after night, stubbornly refused to translate into pop success. Could it really be just down to the lack of a slush fund for payola? More likely there was another factor – the white market still regarded black records as novelty items. Yes to Jimmy Reed's 'Shame Shame Shame', no to Turner's street-wise, urgent 'Gonna Have Fun'.

However, he continued to hedge his bets with greater luck by putting out other records credited to The Ikettes, also now leased to Modern. In 1965 'Peaches 'n' Cream', with Jessie Smith singing lead, climbed to number 36 in the pop charts, and The Ikettes also charted with 'I'm So Thankful' later in the year.

'Peaches 'n' Cream' was a deliberately frothy attempt, cut to orders, to appeal to the white pop market. Turner was dismissive: 'Blacks don't want to hear no shit like that.' He was right, because it only took off when he managed to get it played on pop stations, with just a little payola changing hands.

The relationship with the Biharis soured when Turner discovered that the brothers, noting that The Ikettes were commercially a hotter property than the Revue, tried to sign the girls directly, cutting out their writer and producer. And so Turner looked around for another deal. The Ikettes would have been better of with the Biharis, because Turner was ripping them off in turn.

In spite of their success he kept the royalties and continued simply to pay them their Revue wages. And he refused to compromise the Revue by allowing the girls to do personal appearances in their own right – he hired session singers, who had nothing to do with the records, as the 'live' Ikettes. The real Ikettes retaliated by leaving the Revue, intending to strike out on their own, only to discover that Turner owned their name and so could prevent them from capitalising on their success in a way that cut him out. One Ikette remained with the Revue – Ann Thomas, who according to Turner couldn't sing but was very attractive. Eventually she married Turner and had a child by him, but she still couldn't sing.

Although serious chart action was proving elusive, Turner found time in spite of relentless touring commitments to establish himself as a one-man Los Angeles music industry, partly as insurance against getting ripped off by third parties. He set up a booking agency, Spudnik, on moving to LA in order to avoid paying an outsider's percentage, and so he organised the Revue's sweeps around the country himself. Most of the year's work was in and around Los Angeles anyway, and he had all the contacts, and the repetitive pattern elsewhere helped simplify things. Spudnik also acted for visiting musicians seeking local dates.

Turner avoided the need to pay a road manager by the simple means of instructing the musicians to hump their own gear. He didn't need to give away any royalty points to a producer – he'd been one himself since he was a teenager, and he could also work the desk. He had no manager, because he could similarly work a phone.

However, even the most efficient one-man business cannot look after everything, notably children, when there is a gig every night. Turner got lucky when he went into a local record shop in 1963 and spotted music fan and one-time vocal group member Ann Cain, who of course was well aware of who he was.

Cain became in turn the children's nanny, the telephonist and the custodian of the Spudnik operation. She then graduated to being the Revue cashier on the road, checking the body count at the door against the claims of the promoter and collecting the money – at which point another member of the entourage, Rhonda Graam, was hired to take over Cain's original job of looking after the children. Given that Turner was also indulging in his favourite hobby of serial adultery, although of course since he claimed to be unmarried he couldn't be an adulterer, life was a hectic harem.

Like Tina, Ann Cain both attests to Turner's violence – 'I saw him stick a cigarette up her nose,' confirmation of the dangers of smoking – and yet stayed with him. She became part of the harem, as did Graam, as well as being a staff member of the Revue business. Tina had an obvious reason for putting up with Turner for as long as she could bear it – the children – but since he clearly had the charisma to inspire loyalty in others, in spite of lamentable behaviour, he begins at this time to take on the aura of a religious cult leader. Manson, Jones, Koresh – and, in the rock 'n' roll temple, Turner, a charismatic bad guy.

Quoted in *I, Tina*, Graam – who is white – gives a darker clue to this apparent loyalty. 'You lived in such fear… You wanted to get out, but you were afraid to… If somebody did leave, Ike would always track them down… Ike just couldn't handle rejection.'

After falling out with the Biharis Turner signed with Loma, a quasi-independent R&B label under the Warner Brothers umbrella. Loma boss Bob Krasnow cut an album's-worth of material with Ike and Tina but none of the resulting singles charted.

'River Deep, Mountain High'

'River Deep, Mountain High' is one of the most extraordinary records ever made, a product of Phil Spector's arrogance, obsessiveness and tin ears. He loaded the new four-track tape at LA's Gold Star studios with noise, pushed everything on to one track and hurled more noise at it, reduced it yet again and summoned more noise. If a piece of magnetic tape could bleed at the eardrums, this is it.

Spinal Tap were proud of their amplifiers that went beyond the '10' setting to '11'. Link Wray sometimes gave the impression that his amp *started* at '11'. But Spector, knowing that the sound would be seeping out of tiny transistor radios, went still further. Nearly forty years of technological innovation later, nothing has matched this mad, cluttered scream of a disc created by a demented inventor, the man who believed the press cuttings telling him he was a genius.

Spector got fed up with the fractious Righteous Brothers and they left, signing with Verve. In autumn 1965 he took a job as 'musical supervisor' on a television rock special called *The TNT Show*. This was a follow-up to *The TAMI Show*, later renamed *Gather No Moss* to capitalise on the participation of The Rolling Stones, which was successful enough to graduate to cinema distribution.

Among those Spector had at his disposal were Bo Diddley, Ray Charles, The Ronettes, Joan Baez, The Lovin' Spoonful, The Byrds, Donovan and, as a late addition from the substitutes' bench when an act dropped out, Ike and Tina Turner. In spite of this remarkable roster, and Spector's participation, the show never gelled as well as its predecessor, but it did bring Spector and Tina Turner together. He had already seen her in a Revue performance at a

Sunset Boulevard club, and in his opinion 'they were just sensational'. He began to hatch a plan to top his magisterial Righteous Brothers hit 'You've Lost That Lovin' Feeling'.

Spector was well aware of Ike Turner's reputation as a control freak with a mysterious power over Tina, a rival producer who would want to meddle, but he was determined to work with Tina. And so with Loma's Bob Krasnow acting as middle man Spector offered Turner an irresistible $20,000 up front as long as he, Spector, had total say over the production – he didn't want Turner as a collaborator or as a musician. Indeed, the deal was that Turner wasn't even to attend the sessions. But Turner secured the insurance of an 'Ike and Tina' billing, and in the words of Bud Dain of Liberty Records, quoted in *Rolling Stone*, Spector offered Turner 'an absolute guarantee of hits forever'.

He chose the husband-and-wife team who had written several early Spector hits, Jeff Barry and Ellie Greenwich, to work the magic. Until he met them again he didn't know that they were now divorced, and as the writing process grew intense this occasionally caused tension. 'Every time we'd write a love line, Ellie would start to cry,' he says in Richard Williams's Spector biography *Out of His Head*.

The song gradually grew upwards from its thumping, floor-shaking bass line and its metaphor of a rag doll and a little puppy, childish tokens that would contrast dramatically with Tina's spine-tingling and mature vocal force. The three writers worked together for a fortnight, completing 'I Can Hear Music' and several other songs as well as the mould-breaking 'River Deep'. Tina loved the song. 'For the first time in my life,' she said, 'it wasn't just R&B – it had structure, it had a melody.' She was beginning to tire of screaming over Turner's R&B riffs, and it was her singing voice Spector wanted, not her shouting.

Spector and his arranger Jack Nitzsche then began to lay down the basic tracks but the process went on and on, Spector constantly returning to the studio to crush an extra effect into the mix, burning up an album's-worth of cash on a single side. The musicians included Glen Campbell, Hal Blaine and Leon Russell among at least fifty who were crowded into the room at one stage. Tina went alone to Spector's mansion (with hindsight a brave move) and for a week she rehearsed the complex melody and phrasing for the song. It was 'the first time I'd been given the freedom [by Ike] to go anywhere alone.' Because of his deal with Spector, Turner had no choice. While the backing track was being assembled she only attended the studio once, to lay down a guide vocal, and then on 7 March 1966 she sang it for real.

The b-side was a routine rocker called 'I'll Keep You Happy'. They also cut a stunning, wall-of-sound revival of the Holland-Dozier-Holland classic 'A Love Like Yours (Don't Come Knocking Every Day)', a Barry-Greenwich number 'Hold On Baby', the majestic 'I'll Never Need More Than This' and further covers in Pomus-Shuman's 'Save the Last Dance for Me' and Arthur Alexander's 'Every Day I Have to Cry'. When the tracks were used on a UK *River Deep, Mountain High* album the effect was diluted because the running time was padded out with Turner retreads of old Ike and Tina numbers.

Spector regarded 'River Deep' as his finest hour. Even Turner, who had been kept in the dark throughout, was hugely impressed when he heard the results. Spector posed for publicity pictures with both Ike and Tina, as befitted the billing, and Philles Records – basically Spector and his assistant Danny Davis – took out a *Billboard* trade advertisement. 'Philles Records recently added the dynamic duo, Ike and Tina Turner, to their roster. The couple's first release, entitled "River Deep, Mountain High", was produced by Philles prexy [*Billboard*-speak for president] Phil Spector. In addition, the Philles label acquired The Ikettes, whose release will be forthcoming soon.'

It wasn't, and as is well known but still hard to believe, 'River Deep' bombed in America. This reflected the jinx on Spector's greatest album, *A Christmas Gift For You*, released in November 1963 just when John F Kennedy was assassinated, and aimed at a Christmas market that suddenly didn't feel like buying records.

Maybe American disc-jockeys and programmers decided it was payback time for Spector's conceit, eccentricity, lack of co-operation and refusal to hand out payola. 'People just didn't care for it,' he shrugged, but he was deeply wounded and virtually retired into seclusion. Turner had another theory – Tina was categorised as an R&B artist and so didn't get airplay on pop stations, but the record was pop and so was neglected by R&B stations.

Jeff Barry expressed disappointment in the

production because he felt that it buried his song. He described it as an 'ego record' and indeed it was – monumental ego, monumental record. Not in the American charts, though – in May, after lukewarm reviews, it appeared at number 98, limped as high as number 88 and disappeared. In the UK, however, thanks to the efforts of Decca plugger Tony Hall and the fact that British DJs could hear the record for what it was, without any baggage of resentment for its creator, it reached number 2.

The Rolling Stones enthused about the record, and booked the Revue, along with The Yardbirds, as support act on a Stones tour of the UK running from late September into October 1966. Turner had to recruit another Ikettes line-up, Maxine Smith, Gloria Scott and PP Arnold. The Revue was also booked into ballrooms, clubs and pubs in its own right, on the back of the record's success, in between Stones dates, while new Ikette Arnold was pursued by both Turner and Mick Jagger.

After the tour the Turners did promotional work on the European mainland, and it was at this time that Tina began to think seriously about leaving Turner. She realised that she loved the UK and Europe, offering an escape

route, and she could not take the violence and
the serial adultery much longer. She formed an
affection for a new member of the Revue, baritone sax player Johnny Williams, and while this
was a comfort to her she claims that they did
not have a physical relationship. Williams did
not last long with the band, in any case, so put
off was he by Turner's violent and erratic
behaviour.

One of the most convincing testimonies in *I,
Tina* comes from a casualty-department nurse
in a hospital near to the Turner home in Los
Angeles, since the accounts of violence in the
couple's autobiographies not surprisingly differ
so much that one sometimes wonder if Tina is
exaggerating. 'She would come in in pretty bad
shape, all beat-up and bruised, face swollen,
bloody noses [sic], hematoma on the eyes, all
puffed out and black… ' says Nathan
Schulsinger. But in *Takin' Back My Name*
Turner calls as witness Ronald Bell, from their
UK record company EMI, who says – although
he is not quoted directly – that he never saw evidence of bruising on Tina.

Moving On

The Rolling Stones had helped to open up Europe to the Revue, and so the touring pattern now changed to incorporate it into the regular itinerary in the autumn, with a nightly fee of up to $10,000. When they played at the Royal Albert Hall, reviewer Bill Millar noted, the line-up was pianist Leon Blue, bassist Lee Miles, guitarist Odell Stokes, drummer Howell Portier, and a four-piece brass section of Eddie Burks (trombone), Jimmy Reed (baritone sax), Gerald Gray (tenor sax) and David Hines (trumpet). At this point the Ikettes consisted of Pat Powdrill, Jean Brown, Paulette Parker and Ann Thomas.

Back home, too, the hard work on the road

was paying off, and in 1968 the Revue got its first booking in Las Vegas, at the International Hotel. In May 1969 Ike and Tina returned to the charts with a revival of Otis Redding's 'I've Been Loving You Too Long'. This was taken from a new 'back to the roots' album, *Outta Season*, largely devoted to revivals of blues and R&B classics. In the pop charts the record climbed to number 68, the highest they had been since 1962.

Turner had now moved the act to the Blue Thumb label. Bob Krasnow, who had gone from Loma to Buddah and was now an independent producer, was at the controls. Together they swiftly cut another album, *The Hunter*, which spawned further hits in the title track and the storming dance number 'Bold Soul Sister', which reached 93 and 59 respectively. As a commercial force, Ike and Tina Turner had never been stronger – more prestigious gigs, and back in the charts – even though their relationship off stage was effectively over.

By now Turner, who had never previously dabbled in drugs, was developing his cocaine habit. Bob Krasnow may have been unwittingly responsible, observing to Turner that 'one thing that's good about coke is that you can stay hard

– you can fuck for years behind that stuff'. Turner would have found that prospect irresistible. According to Krasnow he bought his first supply from the saxophonist King Curtis but was ripped off: 'That's no coke, that's Drano!'

In the recollection of his business manager at the time, Ann Cain, it was New Orleans rock 'n' roller Larry Williams who introduced Turner to cocaine. Williams had become a jet-set drug dealer, and in later years claimed to have regretted turning Turner on to the drug, saying that he'd been a nice man until he started using it. Williams, who in January 1980 was found in his Laurel Canyon house with a bullet in his head, had a generous definition of 'nice'. Krasnow compared Turner on drugs to James Brown: 'They're both fucking animals.'

In November 1969 The Rolling Stones arrived in America for a tour beginning at the Los Angeles Forum and, once again, Ike and Tina were on the bill, along with BB King. At Tina's insistence they had a new number in their repertoire, John Lennon's 'Come Together'. The feeling she had about 'River Deep, Mountain High', that it was broadening her range beyond 12-bar R&B, was now leading her towards rock songs – as well as 'Come Together' she picked up on the Stones' 'Honky Tonk Women' and Credence Clearwater Revival's 'Proud Mary' among other recent hits.

Tina's dynamic interpretation of 'Come Together' was now a highlight of the act, a show-stopper on the Stones' tour. 'I've Been Loving You Too Long' was another, with Tina caressing the microphone and simulating sex while Ike groaned in the background.

The final night was at the West Palm Beach Pop Festival, after which the Stones – but not Ike and Tina – moved on to play a hastily arranged free concert at the Altamont Speedway just outside San Francisco. In an attempt to avoid trouble, the notorious local Hell's Angels were employed as stewards. The tragic events that unfolded – four deaths, including the murder of a young black man, Meredith Hunter, by Angels just in front of the stage – brought the Swinging Sixties to a grim close. The tour and its awful climax was filmed as a cinema documentary by the Maysles brothers, Albert and David, and was released as *Gimme Shelter*.

Early in 1970 Turner hopped labels once

more to Minit, a small R&B imprint under the umbrella of Liberty/United Artists. 'Come Together', with 'Honky Tonk Women' making up a stunning double-sider, entered the charts in March and reached number 57. In August the follow-up, now on the parent Liberty label, was even more successful. It was another cover version, this time 'I Want to Take You Higher', originally by Sly and the Family Stone, and it went to number 34. The deal with Minit reportedly guaranteed Turner $50,000 a year but the label soon defaulted, leaving him free to sign with Liberty for three times that amount.

Halfway through his second year on Liberty he succeeded in persuading them to advance a further $150,000. By now he had also developed Chuck Berry's habit of insisting on upfront payments for gigs and TV appearances – he turned up for an Ed Sullivan Show seemingly without his guitar, explaining that he needed the 'key' for it – cash. He got it.

In spite of the fact that he was now rolling in money he remained a mean employer – one Ikette claimed that the girls were paid $30 a night within fifty miles of Los Angeles with an extra $5 further away, and from that they had to find their own accommodation as well as risking fines like $10 for a laddered stocking. Another claimed that The Ikettes had actually written 'Bold Soul Sister' themselves, but that Turner claimed the credit and paid them $15 each for the session.

An exception to his stinginess would occur when he wanted to sleep with one of them. 'It was very common to get approached by Ike,' said one. 'He'd be shrewd about it, buy you things and make you think twice about it.'

He had a kind of fetish about banknotes, combined with a carelessness, a confidence that more cash would magically appear. 'He came into the front room at Blue Thumb,' Krasnow recalled, 'and threw $70,000 on the floor, in cash, and dared anyone to touch it. Just to blow everybody's mind.'

In December 1970 Ike and Tina went into a studio in Florida and cut their full-tilt revival of 'Proud Mary'. It was the biggest US hit of their career, peaking at number 4 in late January 1971. Tina's impulse to persuade Ike to let her record these rock covers was a personal one – her musical tastes were broadening all the time – but it had incidentally unlocked the door to a scale of commercial success that could never have been reached by Turner's more purist devotion to blues and R&B. By now he was a very rich man – even more so because during their annual season in Las Vegas he proved to be that rarity, a successful gambler.

Turner's natural home was the recording studio, and now he could afford his own purpose-built room. Two rooms, in fact – he bought a property near his mansion, at 1310 La Brea Avenue, and converted it into two studios, a large one for renting out and a smaller set-up for his own use. He called the building Bolic Sound. The desk in the control room cost $90,000, complete with the latest innovations like a computerised 'mix memoriser'. Naturally there was also an apartment for parties, dominated by a mural that might well have met with Saddam Hussain's approval – a kitsch, life-size, realistic depiction of a naked couple embracing in the surf.

An anonymous member of Turner's entourage observed that with heavy cocaine use came paranoia. 'You got to think that somebody was watching you all the time. And of course somebody *was*. There was a TV camera trained on every room.' Turner could sit at his control desk and flick from camera to camera, spying on everyone, including when they were entertaining groupies.

In a *Rolling Stone* feature for the 14th October issue, Ben Fong-Torres describes Turner's house in all its striking vulgarity – the television in a whale-shaped cabinet, an indoor waterfall, ceiling mirrors, a gold-plated angel holding a torch, a coffee table in the shape of a bass guitar. Bob Krasnow's reaction has become legend: 'You mean you can actually spend $70,000 at Woolworth's?'

In the piece Tina recalls their early days on stage together. 'Ike used to move on stage. He was bow-legged and bow-hipped and when he moved from side to side, he had an effect he used to do with the guitar, and I used to do that, 'cause I idolised him so.'

She also explains the involvement of Mick Jagger in booking the Revue as support for the Stones. 'Mick was a friend of Phil Spector... [He], I guess, thought the record was great, and he caught our act a couple of times... he was excited about our show, and he thought it'd be different for the people in England.' Tina also claims to have inspired Jagger's characteristic stage posturing.

Her first reaction to Turner's studio was, 'Wonderful – I'll be rid of him.' But he soon started summoning her from the house at all hours of the night to add her vocals to whatever he and the band had been working on, and when she got to the studio everyone would invariably be stoned and incoherent. She seemed to be tied to him now only by fear, with no love left. Indeed, she could form a friendship with his main mistress Ann Thomas – they were close because they were trapped in the same situation.

Late in 1971 Turner cut an album at Bolic called *Strange Fruit*, which was released on United Artists. It was cumbersomely credited to Ike Turner Presents... The Family Vibes, which the sleeve reveals as the new name of the Kings of Rhythm. Ten musicians are shown on the gatefold, wearing the sort of clothes that have not stood the test of time. The resulting doodlings are pleasant enough as background music but it is indicative that the strongest track is also the most conventional, a straightforward boogie-woogie called 'Bootie Lip'. As for the rest, it appears to show what talented blues, soul and funk musicians can produce if holed up in a studio with unlimited time and unlimited cocaine.

Nutbush City Limits

It wasn't long after the opening of the studio that Turner was in trouble with the police, but not through drugs. He had installed an illegal gadget, a 'blue box', that enabled him to dial another number, press a button, and thus re-route all further call charges to that number – ideally an office exchange where the deception would be harder to spot. He used it for his booking agency, but the phone company got wise to it and alerted the police. Turner's lawyer managed to limit the punishment to a few thousand dollars.

In spite of the long, stoned hours spent in the

studio, the Revue's commercial appeal dipped once again in the early 70s. Two albums, *Nuff Said* and *Feel Good*, were comparative failures, and early in 1972 the single 'Up in Heah' stalled at number 83.

Just as it was Tina's broadening tastes, unacknowledged by Turner, that had indirectly given their career such a heady boost in the late 1960s, so it was her newfound songwriting abilities that provided them with one last smash hit. A song about her home town in Tennessee, 'Nutbush City Limits', reached number 22 in November 1973. In the UK it almost equalled 'River Deep, Mountain High', peaking at number 4. With its squelchy, insistent guitar riff and a strutting rhythm perfectly suited to Tina's foot-stomping, wide-thighed stage style, it was a rock 'n' roll antidote to a musical world that at this time was beginning to get a little serious and 'progressive'. It was a clever musical bridge: some modish synthesiser and guitar effects to give it an up-to-date veneer, laid over a pounding track with some satisfying chord changes, and right on top Tina's wonderful, unapproachable voice.

A persistent rumour that the British glam-rocker Marc Bolan played on 'Nutbush' was eventually confirmed by Tina in a BBC radio interview. Bolan certainly had the musical qualifications – his style, however dressed up it might have been with feather boas, eye make-up and hippy sentiments, was firmly rooted in Howlin' Wolf and Chuck Berry.

But this success was, of course, too late to save their relationship, even though Tina took a long time to make the break. The drugs, the violence and the infidelity had driven Tina to attempt suicide on more than one occasion, but escape was eventually to arrive – following a bruising beating – in positive rather than tragic form.

Going over to London to film her part as the Acid Queen in Ken Russell's adaptation of Pete Townshend's 'rock opera' *Tommy* was to be a significant step towards liberation and eventual superstardom. The film was released in 1975, the same year as Ike and Tina Turner's last-gasp minor hit, 'Baby Get It On'. In the meantime Tina had cut her first solo album, a country collection recorded at Bolic, though not produced by Turner, called *Tina Turns the Country On*, and the duo had their penultimate, and again modest, hit 'Sexy Ida (Part One)'.

Again, though without Tina's confirmation

this time, Marc Bolan is said to be playing on both 'Sexy Ida' and 'Baby Get It On'. Indeed, Bolan himself once went so far as to claim authorship of 'Nutbush' and 'Sexy Ida'. The most likely bet is that he is indeed on all three, and had some in-studio input into the songs.

Between 'Nutbush' and their final break-up in 1976 bookings for the Revue declined and Turner's coke habit worsened. It had already eaten away the inside of his nose, causing pain that could only be frozen with another snort. He began to descend into befuddled obscurity just as the graph of Tina's career began to climb and climb. He became more and more reclusive, plotting to less and less effect in his Inglewood fortress.

In an interview with Dominick A Miserandino, Turner excused his behaviour. 'All at once, money was coming from everywhere, everybody knows you, you're super-popular. Girls pulling at you everywhere from every angle. People smiling at you with phony smiles. Then I was introduced to drugs: cocaine, that's all I ever done. Then I started having a lot of cocaine around me and that drew even more phony people... It all came too fast, man, and I didn't know how to handle it.'

It came so fast that it took thirty years to arrive. As self-justification it sounds thin. Turner had always been a womaniser, and took to drugs with enthusiasm to enhance his performance. The idea that he could be duped by false friends is somewhat ludicrous. Ian McLagan of The Faces recalls the contemporary scene *chez* Turner.

'In March 1974 we were in Los Angeles on tour. After a gig we'd often go to The Record Plant hanging out with Bobby Womack. The sessions were actually Jim Keltner's – they'd been going on for ever and there were lots of people coming and going. One night we were warming up backstage at The Forum when Mick Jagger came in. Then Bobby Womack turned up – so everyone who'd recorded 'It's All Over Now' was in the room. Bobby wrote it with his sister Shirley and recorded it in 1964 with his group, The Valentinos. The Stones covered it and their version overtook Bobby's on the charts. Then Rod [Stewart] did another cover on *Gasoline Alley*. All together.

'Once we'd done the gig Mick suggested we look in on Ike Turner at his recording studio. We didn't need persuading – I'd been a fan of Ike and Tina since "It's Gonna Work Out Fine", and we did "Too Much Woman For a Hen-Pecked Man" in our set. So we were in the limo and rolled up at this place Bolic Sound. I thought, surely he must have heard of the word "Bollocks"? I forgot to ask him!

'This was in Inglewood, not a place you'd want to hang about in. But we didn't have much choice. We waited outside while these video cameras watched us. At long last a door opened into a long corridor, security gates at both ends, and now it was armed guards watching us. I thought, Fort Ike! It was Mick who could open the doors for us, and fortunately it got through that he was with us. We were allowed into the corridor and had to wait again at the other end for more clearance.

'Then we got as far as the kitchen area. Ike was chatting up a couple of girls – Tina wasn't around. Mick introduced us and Ike, who was very friendly to us, gave us the guided tour. He took us to his office, sat down at the desk and pointed to a big silver ornament in the form of a crab.

'"First things first," he said. The shell lifted back and there was all this Peruvian flake in the crab. He had a silver chain around his neck. He took it off and hanging from it was a double-headed silver snake. The hollowed-out heads were spoons. He scooped up the coke and snorted it, one nostril and then the next. He passed round the snake to everyone.

'Then Mick mentioned "Rocket 88". Ike leaped up and pulled a piano out of the wall – it was like a foldaway bed. He played for us – it was stunning. Then he continued the tour. There was a guest suite, very elaborate decorations, four-poster bed, TV nearly up in the ceiling, thick carpets.

'He switched on the television and there was this short, grainy video showing. I saw a little camera above the bed, and suddenly I remembered an Ike and Tina album in a gatefold cover. On the inside was a grainy picture of Tina sprawling on a four-poster bed. This one! He invited us to stay but I wasn't having any of that. Starring in one of his movies.

'When he got as far as the studio Tina arrived. She looked pissed off with him. She was very nice to us, but she seemed uncomfortable – it was like Ike's territory. She didn't stay long.

'Then Ike set us up with instruments and we began to jam. But gradually Ike took charge, interrupting, giving orders. He took over the piano from me and showed me what he wanted. Then he disappeared into the control room. I wasn't enjoying it any more. We were now playing one of Ike's tunes, and he'd manoeuvred it so that we were acting as his session band! I felt trapped – there was no coke in sight and Mick had disappeared. I've always reckoned that he saw what was happening and slipped away back to the hotel. We didn't escape until eight in the morning, by which time it had become a total drag.'

One thing that emerges from Mac's recollections is the parallel with Phil Spector's creepy mansion. Two coked-up, self-centred musical geniuses, each surrounding himself in a plush, vulgar, artificially-lit cocoon of indulgence and paranoia. At least The Faces got out alive.

Break Up

After filming *Tommy* Tina, still in London, was a guest star on an Ann-Margret TV special, filmed for screening in America, another step towards independence. They sang 'Proud Mary', 'Nutbush City Limits' and 'Honky Tonk Women' together. Turner, meanwhile, spent most of his time in the studio, which now had a 32-track desk, trying out ideas and altering them time after time. 'Ike got worse,' Tina recalls. 'You never knew what you were getting hit for.'

In June 1975 Ike and Tina had their last hit, 'Baby Get It On', which only climbed to number 88. Tina tried to escape Ike – she went to stay with a cousin, but he found her and beat her up.

She ran away again and stayed in hiding for two weeks. Then she returned to tell Turner that she was leaving for good. First, though, there was one last tour to go through, beginning on the Fourth of July, 1976. The first booking was at the Hilton in Dallas.

When they arrived there Turner became violent once more, and by Tina's account she was very badly cut and bruised. She waited until Turner fell asleep in their room, and she ran for it. She had just 36 cents and no luggage, but the manager of another hotel took pity on her and let her stay. She called Turner's lawyer, which she knew was risky but she had few options, and he arranged to get her back to Los Angeles, where she stayed with various friends.

Turner was again holed up in his studio, in theory working on a solo album. A blues collection did eventually appear. He found out where Tina was staying but now he changed his tactics. Instead of storming over and dragging her away, he sent the children to her and gave her $1,000 to rent somewhere. Tina guessed that he was gambling that when that tiny allowance was exhausted she would be forced to come back. She was determined not to, but as yet her name meant little as a solo attraction, and in the meantime the promotors involved in the aborted tour were chasing her with breach-of-contract writs – it was her, after all, who had defaulted.

Tina, with the help of Turner's former business manager Rhonda Graam, booked herself on to any television show that would have her, eking out a meagre living and slowly paying her debts. And on 27th July 1976 she filed for divorce, citing 'irreconcilable differences'. She found a lawyer, Arthur Leeds, and indicated that she was not willing to hassle for half of Turner's assets – all she wanted was freedom together with modest alimony and child allowance payments. She then secured a solo deal with United Artists, with sufficient funds up front to organise a tour. She was now out on her own.

She still found it hard to shake Turner off, however. When she got hold of some publishing royalties she moved the family again, but Turner found out where she was. Presumably as a warning that he was still watching her, a car parked outside her house had its windows shot out and was set on fire. It belonged to the girl-friend of Craig, Tina's son. Tina had no doubt who was responsible, though Turner claims that it was someone who thought they were doing him a favour. This in spite of the fact that he admits driving around looking for her with a loaded gun, intent on frightening her.

Turner was still fighting her through the lawyers, as well. He was attacking on two fronts – firstly, that they had never actually married, and secondly, that by leaving she had deprived him of income from his main asset, Ike and Tina Turner. Naturally, Turner also made unrealistically modest assessments of his other assets, notably the value of his real estate. By the autumn of 1977, now beginning to make a name for herself, Tina tired of all the hassle and she withdrew from the legal wrangling. So Turner got to keep pretty well everything that had been built up as a result of their joint popularity. The divorce was finalised on 29th March 1978. Turner reflected elegantly on Tina's wish to break free. 'She was just tired of the embarrassment of being Mrs Turner when I was travelling with four women and fucking all four of them.'

He issued an album on United Artists called *Airwaves*, and credited it to Ike and Tina Turner. It consisted of their last work together, but it failed commercially. Although Turner no longer had the expense of keeping a band on the road he was running short of money. Just in time, an investment he had made in some Canadian oil-wells began to realise a profit, and he also had property interests that started to provide a regular rental income.

In a 1999 interview with Michael Shelden of *The Miami Herald* Turner was unrepentant. 'Tina exaggerates about me beating her,' he claims. 'Have you seen how big she is? Man, she could handle bigger guys than me if she wanted to. But ain't it part the woman's fault if she stays around and lets me hit her? She didn't have to put up with that.'

He then makes a distinction between hitting, which he admits, and beating, which he denies. So it was Tina's fault for staying, and anyway she was unable to tell the crucial difference between hitting and beating.

In Turner's defence, the fan who attempted to put a little order into Turner's rambling autobiography, Nigel Cawthorne, points quite reasonably to an inaccuracy in the film *What's Love Got To Do With It?*. The movie, he says, 'portrays Ike as a huge man dominating the petite Tina. Look at any of their early album covers. He is small and wiry – she is the one carrying the meat.'

But Cawthorne also admits: 'This is not to say that Ike is Mr Nice Guy. He has a volcanic temper and can be scary to be with.' He is also very demanding – biographer Cawthorne became Turner's unwilling assistant, valet and general factotum, his 'acolyte'. 'I stood just a couple of months of this,' he says. 'How did Tina manage eighteen years?'

Without a band, without Tina – whom he had relied on for her dog-like support however badly he treated her – Turner was finding life meaningless, just a round of coke-snorting and musical doodlings that usually came to nothing. In spite of his virtuosity on piano and guitar he was above all a musical organiser, a visionary, and now he had nothing to organise. He was also well aware of his vocal limitations and – this invariably seems surprising in such a tempestuous personality – his shyness on stage. 'I just went into a fifteen-year party,' is how he puts it.

Throughout all this, however, one person from the old entourage had remained faithful, Ann Thomas. They married in Las Vegas on 11th April 1981, but of course it did not last. A further solo album emerged from Turner's long, stoned sojourns at Bolic, but in 1982 the studio

was destroyed by fire. Turner did not record
again until 2000.

The Wilderness and Back

The remainder of the 1980s passed without Turner noticing it much. 'How much money did I spend on cocaine?' he said in a 2001 interview with Caroline Graham for the *Mail on Sunday* magazine *Night and Day*. 'Probably $11million. If I had my time again I'd have stashed some of it away, I can tell you. But I didn't know any better. I was young and hot-headed and out to have a good time.' And when he wasn't snorting cocaine he was drinking hard, incapable of work, living on his investments and royalties.

In the meantime, in 1986, Tina Turner became a superstar. Her album *Private Dancer* went platinum and in the following fourteen years until her retirement from touring in 2000 she sold over 75 million albums and was one of the biggest-grossing concert attractions in the world. She published *I, Tina*, which awoke the world to the abuse she suffered at Turner's hands, and this in turn led to the 1993 film *What's Love Got To Do With It?*

If he had not been busted for cocaine possession in 1989 Turner would presumably be dead by now. In 1990 he was sentenced to eighteen months. He reckons he was lucky – the police found a modest amount of coke but missed all the rest and a small arsenal of guns. Before he went to prison Turner was aware of the risks he was taking by using cocaine, but as an addict he could not get clean, could never quite face cold turkey. Now, after constant brushes with the law, he found himself in jail. He was so frightened of the dangers and privations of life in prison that he was, to quote the title of a movie on the subject, 'scared straight'. 'I was so damn scared... I didn't do any drugs.' When he was surrounded by cocaine he could never resist it, but suddenly he found it easy. He told *Night and Day*: 'I cleaned up my act and started thinking about life.'

But his childhood experience of making a

living by street hustling came in handy. By behaving himself he became a 'trustee' prisoner, and this gave him access to the prison shop. He bought chocolate bars and other sweets, then cigarettes and coffee, and sold them to fellow inmates at a profit. 'I was making $500 a day when I was in jail,' he claims. While he was inside Ike and Tina were inducted into The Rock 'n' Roll Hall of Fame, in January 1991, and he was released in September.

In 1993 he had a huge slice of luck, and a second one he could have done without. The bad luck was the movie, inevitably reaching more people than Tina's book, reviving the wife-beating image. The Disney studio paid him $45,000 for the right to represent him in the film, but of course he had no control over how he was characterised. 'The worst deal I ever did,' he told *Night and Day*. 'They didn't show any of the good stuff about Ike and Tina, just the negative shit. I couldn't get work anywhere. I was branded a wife-beater. Was some of that true? Yes. Was that all Ike and Tina were about? No.'

Having admitted to the slaps and punches, he then says something that stretches one's credulity too far. 'I did no more to Tina than I would mind someone doing to my mother in the same circumstances.'

The lack of work suddenly became insignificant, however. The rappers Salt-N-Pepa were hot at the time, and they sampled his 1962 Ikettes track 'I'm Blue' on their huge hit 'Shoop'. It made him a quarter of a million, although in one quote that figure was tripled, and bought him a house in San Marcos, south of Los Angeles, and a Mercedes. He furnished the house with his characteristic lack of taste, as if a cut-price Michael Jackson had been hired as the interior decorator. And he built himself another studio. The rehabilitation was underway, and for him the modest house represented 'my fresh start'.

He had to make a further fresh start if he wanted to get back into music properly, and that was as a front man on stage. 'All my life I was afraid to come out front,' he told writer Eric Snider. 'I don't know whether I was afraid or bashful. I liked it better in the background.'

Having steeled himself, he found that he was accepted. His audience may have believed the movie, but he was still a phenomenal pianist and guitar player, enough to overcome both his reputation and the limitations of his vocal style.

'Now I've got the nerve to go on stage and play everything that comes outta my head,' he says of this rebirth.

Turner put together a new version of the Kings of Rhythm. In *Juke Blues* Brian Baumgartner reviewed a 1997 return to Clarksdale for the Sunflower River Blues & Gospel festival. 'Ike opened the set on keyboards. He somehow managed to make it sound like a real piano, doing a rocking version of "Rocket 88". He switched over to guitar after about three numbers and with The Ikettes hitting the stage in the tightest fitting outfits imaginable, gave the hometown audience a storming 1960s R&B show.' A photograph taken at the gig confirms the description of The Ikettes' dresses, which appear to have come out of an aerosol.

As well as running his own band again, he teamed up with bluesman Joe Louis Walker. 'Ike, I'll pay you $5,000 a night and you don't have to do but six songs,' Walker reportedly told him. 'Well, that money sounded pretty good,' said Turner. He also found a 'new Tina' and partner in Audrey Madison, although he now appears to have sworn off marriage, real or otherwise.

The final mark of rehabilitation was Turner's 2001 recording *Here and Now*, slowly built up over a period of four years, which proves that the fire still burns. He assembled the arrangements, style and tempo of each song on the computer before turning them over to the musicians. It is a solo album owing nothing to the Ike and Tina Revue. 'The reason I never did it before was that I was just afraid of rejection,' he told Rod Harmon of the Knight Rider News Service. 'I didn't have any confidence in me. I had confidence in my ability to put it together.' But out front, there would always be Tina, or Billy Gayles, or Jackie Brenston.

It was Cilla Huggins of *Juke Blues* who first suggested to Turner that he should return to his roots in jump blues. 'That would be going backwards,' was his first reaction. But when he joined Joe Louis Walker's show he realised that it was actually his strength. At the age of 70 he could not be a contemporary pop star, and he could not be half of Ike and Tina. 'The more I did it,' he said, referring to his return to the music he used to play, 'the better I loved it.' And so with Rob Johnson of Bottled Majic Music he put together *Here and Now*.

Most of the tracks were recorded at his San

Marcos studio, with others cut live at EVEJIM Studio in Los Angeles. Among the studios used for overdubbing was Willie Mitchell's legendary set-up in Memphis, Tennessee. The album involved reunions with two musicians from the past – his childhood friend from Clarksdale, Ernest Lane, played piano on several tracks, while Little Milton added his distinctive guitar to a couple.

A stomping revival of 'I'm Tore Up', the Kings of Rhythm number cut for Federal in 1956, with Billy Gayles out front, sets the mood. Turner's lissom guitar lines decorate the song, and his voice is judiciously bolstered with echo. 'Baby's Got It' is an up-tempo piano piece with driving brass figures, and the sensuous rhythm of 'You Can't Winnum All' is topped by Little Milton's guitar. The song is a rejigged version of Jackie Brenston's 1958 Cobra side 'You've Got To Lose'. 'Ike's Theme' is a slinky guitar workout that recalls 'Grumbling' from 1968, and it has an inevitable helping of Turner's tremolo effect, his 'whammy bar'.

'Catfish Blues', one of the tracks featuring Lane, is an effective version of the classic Delta blues. Of 'Gave You What You Wanted' Turner comments: 'That's when I first started to use the whammy bar again.' This is a slow blues with a vocal both meditative and menacing, while 'I Need A-Nuddin' is lighter in mood, with a strutting rhythm and a touch of New Orleans funk. 'Swanee River Boogie' is a virtuoso piece, a piano *tour de force* that sets up a relentless Jerry Lee Lewis rhythm, states the theme simply and humourously and then turns it loose. It has its origins in the old Albert Ammons version that Turner became familiar with as a child, hearing it as the theme song to one of the shows on Nashville radio station WLAC.

By contrast, 'Feelin' Low Down' is an echo-drenched improvised blues adorned by a weeping Little Milton solo, and 'Rocket 88' is a joyful return to the song that started the legend. It has a swaggering rhythm and Turner's vocal simply rides along with it, rather than trying to compete with Jackie Brneston's rollicking style. The album is completed by a sombre blues workout, 'Cold Day in Hell'.

Here and Now is convincing evidence of a rehabilitated Ike Turner, both musically and in that he has turned his back, just in time, on a violent and destructive lifestyle. To a degree he had to relearn his skills. When the idea of the album was first mooted, he says, 'I went home, and I tried to play "Prancing"... it was like an impossibility. So then I found out what I had lost... I started to get back into learning what I had forgot.'

And of his career he says: 'It's better now than it's ever been.'

Bibliography

I, Tina: My Life Story by Tina Turner with Kurt Loder (Viking, 1986)

Takin' Back My Name: The Confessions of Ike Turner by Ike Turner with Nigel Cawthorne (Virgin, 1999)

Sun Records: The Blues Years 1950-1956 – booklet and liner notes by Colin Escott, Hank Davis, Bez Turner, Martin Hawkins and Rob Bowman (Charly Records)

Ike Turner Starts Over by Kenneth Bays (*Blues Revue*, June 2001)

Juke Blues – various editions, notably Cilla Huggins's 1997 interview with Ike Turner

Rebirth of the Cool by Eric Snider

Ike Turner Making Comeback by Nekesa Mumbi Moody (Associated Press)

What's Love Got To Do With It? By Caroline Graham (*Mail on Sunday*, July 29 2001)

Ike and Tina Turner Discography by Pierre Daguerre, Kurt Mohr and Jacques Perin (*Soul Bag*, October 1976)

Interview with Ike Turner by Margaret Moser, 2001

Joel Whitburn's Top Pop Records 1955-1972 (Record Research, 1973)

British Hit Singles by Paul Gambaccini, Tim Rice and Jonathan Rice (Guinness Publishing, 1993)

Blues Unlimited – various editions

Chuck Berry: The Biography by John Collis (Aurum, 2002)

Interview with Ed Bicknell by John Collis

Concert review by Bill Millar (*Soul Music*, 1966)

Rolling Stone – various editions

Out of his Head: The Sound of Phil Spector by Richard Williams (Abacus, 1974)

The Phil Spector Story by Rob Finnis (Rockon, 1975)

Billboard – various editions

Interview with Ike Turner by Dominick A Miserandino

Correspondence with Ian McLagan

Interview with Ike Turner by Michael Shelden (*The Miami Herald*, 1999)

Discography

Compiled by Fred Rothwell

USA Singles featuring Ike Turner

Jackie Brenston & His Delta Cats
   (Ike plays piano)
   Rocket 88 / Come Back Where You Belong
   Chess 1458
   1951

Ike Turner & His Kings Of Rhythm
   Heartbroken And Worried / I'm Lonesome Baby
   Chess 1459
   1951

Jackie Brenston & His Delta Cats
   (Ike plays piano on A-side)
   My Real Gone Rocket / Tuckered Out
   Chess 1469 – 1951

Jackie Brenston & His Delta Cats
(Ike plays piano on B-side)
Juiced / Independent Woman
Chess 1472
1951

Howlin' Wolf
(Ike plays piano on B-side)
Moanin' At Midnight / How Many More
Years
Chess 1479
1951

Robert (Bobby) Bland
(Ike plays piano)
Dry Up Baby / Crying All Night Long
Modern 848
1951

The Howlin' Wolf
(Ike plays piano on A-side)
Riding In The Moonlight / Moaning At
Midnight
RPM 333
1951

BB King
(Ike plays piano)
Three O'Clock Blues / That Ain't The Way To
Do It
RPM 339
1951

BB King
  (Ike plays piano)
  Story From My Heart And Soul / Boogie
  Woogie Woman
  Modern 374
  1952

Houston Baines
  (Ike plays piano)
  Going Home / Relation Blues
  Blues & Rhythm 7001
  1952

Brother Bell
  (Ike plays piano)
  Whole Heap Of Mama / If You Feel Froggish
  Blues & Rhythm 7002
  1952

Charley Booker
  (Ike plays piano)
  Rabbit Blues / No Ridin' Blues
  Blues & Rhythm 7003
  1952

Little Junior Parker
  (Ike plays piano)
  Bad Women, Bad Whiskey / You're My Angel
  Modern 864
  1952

Bobby "Blue" Bland With Ike Turner Orchestra
(Ike plays piano and guitar)
Good Lovin' (Love You Baby-Love You Yes I Do) / Drifting From Town To Town
Modern 868
1952

Ben Burton Orchestra
(Ike plays piano)
Bee Hive Boogie / Blues And Jam
Modern 871
1952

Charley Booker
(Ike plays piano)
Moonrise Blues / Charley's Boogie Woogie
Modern 878
1952

Mary Sue
(Ike plays piano)
Everybody's Talking / Love Is A Gamble
Modern 880
1952

Baby Face Turner
(Ike plays guitar)
Blue Serenade / Gonna Let You Go
Modern 882
1952

Ben Burton Orchestra
(Ike plays piano)
Lover's Blues / Cherokee Boogie
Modern 894
1952

Elmore James With The Broom Dusters
(Ike plays piano on A-side)
Please Find My Baby / Strange Kinda Feeling
Flair 1022
1953

The Prisonaires
(Ike plays piano)
My God Is Real / Softly And Tenderly
Sun 189
1953

The Prisonaires
(Ike plays guitar on A-side)
A Prisoner's Prayer / I Know
Sun 191
1953

Little Milton
(Ike plays piano)
Beggin' My Baby / Somebody Told Me
Sun 194
1953

Billy "The Kid" Emerson
(Ike plays guitar)

No Teasing Around / If Lovin' Is Believing
Sun 195
1954

Little Milton
(Ike plays piano)
Alone And Blue / If You Love Me Baby
Sun 200
1954

Billy "The Kid" Emerson
(Ike plays guitar)
I'm Not Going Home / The Woodchuck
Sun 203
1954

Raymond Hill
(Ike plays guitar)
The Snuggle / Bourbon Street Jump
Sun 204
1954

Elmore James With The Broom Dusters
(Ike plays piano on A-side)
Hand In Hand / Make My Dream Come True
Flair 1031
1954

Eugene Fox (with Ike Turner)
Stay At Home / Sinners Dream
Checker 792
1954

Jesse Knight & His Combo (with Ike Turner)
Nobody Seems To Want Me / Nothing But
Money
Checker 797
1954

Lover Boy (Ike Turner)
The Way You Used To Treat Me / Love Is Scarce
RPM 409
1954

Lonnie "The Cat" With Bobby Hines Band
(Ike plays piano)
I Ain't Drunk / The Road I Travel
RPM 410
1954

The Fox
(Ike plays piano)
The Dream Pt.1 / The Dream Pt.2
RPM 420
1954

Johnny Wright With The Ike Turner Orchestra
I Stayed Down / ?
Deluxe 6029
1954

Clayton Love
(Ike plays guitar)
Why Don't You Believe In Me / Wicked Little
Baby

Modern 929
1954

Dennis Binder & His Orchestra
(Ike plays piano)
I Miss You So / Early Times
Modern 930
1954

Matt Cockrell
(Ike plays piano)
Baby Please / Gypsy Blues
Flair 1037
1954

Billy Gale & His Orchestra
(Ike plays guitar)
Night Howler / My Heart Is In Your Hands
Flair 1038
1954

Elmore James & His Broom Dusters
(Ike plays piano)
Sho Nuff I Do / 1839 Blues
Flair 1039
1954

Ike Turner & His Orchestra
Loosely / Cubano Jump
Flair 1040
1954

The Flairs
  (Ike plays guitar)
  Baby Wants / You Were Untrue
  Flair 1041
  1954

Elmore James & The Broom Dusters
  (Ike plays piano on A-side)
  Rock My Baby Right / Dark And Dreary
  Flair 1048
  1954

The Sly Fox
  (Ike plays guitar)
  Hoo-Doo Say / I'm Tired Of Beggin'
  Spark 108
  1954

The Sly Fox
  (Ike plays guitar)
  My Four Women / Alley Music
  Spark 112
  1954

Little Milton
  (Ike plays piano)
  Looking For My Baby / Homesick For My
  Baby
  Sun 220
  1955

Ike Turner & His Orchestra
  Cuban Getaway / Go To It
  Flair 1059
  1955

Johnny Wright with Ike Turner's Orchestra
  (Ike plays guitar)
  The World Is Yours / Suffocate
  RPM 443
  1955

The Trojan's
  (Ike plays guitar)
  As Long As I Have You / I Wanna Make Love
  To You
  RPM 446
  1955

Richard Berry with the Ike Turner Orchestra
  Rockin' Man / Big John
  RPM 448
  1955

Willie King with Ike Turner's Band featuring Billy Gayles
  (Ike plays guitar)
  Peg Leg Woman / Mistreating Me
  Vita 123
  1956

Billy Gales with Ike Turner's Rhythm Rockers
  (Ike plays guitar)
  I'm Tore Up / If I Never Had Known You
  Federal 12265
  1956

The Rockers
  (Ike plays guitar)
  What Am I To Do / I'll Die In Love With You
  Federal 12267
  1956

Billy Gales with Ike Turner's Rhythm Rockers
  (Ike plays guitar)
  Let's Call It A Day / Take Your Fine Frame
  Home
  Federal 12272
  1956

The Rockers
  (Ike plays guitar)
  Why Don't You Believe / Down In The Bottom
  Federal 12273
  1956

Billy Gales with Ike Turner's Kings Of Rhythm
  (Ike plays guitar)
  No Coming Back / Do Right Baby
  Federal 12282
  1956

Jackie Brenston With Ike Turner's Kings Of Rhythm
(Ike plays guitar)
What Can It Be / Gonna Wait For My Chance
Federal 12283
1956

The Gardenias
(Ike plays guitar)
Flaming Love / My Baby's Tops
Federal 12284
1956

Billy Gales with Ike Turner's Kings Of Rhythm
(Ike plays guitar)
Sad As A Man Can Be / Just One More Time
Federal 12287
1956

Jackie Brenston with Ike Turner's Kings Of Rhythm
(Ike plays guitar)
Much Later / The Mistreater
Federal 12291
1957

Ike Turner and his Orchestra
(Ike plays guitar)
Do You Mean It / She Made My Blood Run Cold

Federal 12297
1957

Ike Turner and his Orchestra
(Ike plays guitar)
The Big Question / Rock-A-Bucket
Federal 12304
1957

Ike Turner and his Orchestra
(Ike plays guitar)
You've Changed My Love / Trail Blazer
Federal 12307
1957

Ike Turner, Carlson Oliver & Little Ann (A)/Ike Turner Orch. (B)
Box Top / Chalypso Love Cry
Tune Town 501
1958

Kenneth Churchill & The Lyrics with Ike Turner Orchestra
(Ike plays guitar)
Would You Rather / Fate Of Rock And Roll
Joyce 304
1958

Otis Rush & His Band
(Ike plays guitar)
Double Trouble / Keep On Loving Me Baby
Cobra 5030 – 1958

Betty Everett & The Willie Dixon Band
(Ike plays piano on A-side and guitar on B-
side)
I'll Weep No More / Tell Me Darling
Cobra 5031
1958

Otis Rush & His Band
(Ike plays guitar)
All Your Love (I Miss Loving) / My Baby Is A
Good 'Un
Cobra 5032
1958

Ike Turner's Kings Of Rhythm
(Ike plays guitar and piano on A-side and sings
and plays guitar on B-side)
Walking Down The Aisle / Box Top
Cobra 5033
1959

Buddy Guy
(Ike plays guitar on A-side)
You Sure Can't Do / This Is The End
Artistic 1503
1959

Ike Turner's Kings Of Rhythm
(Ike plays piano & guitar)
(I Know) You Don't Love Me / Down And
Out
Artistic 1504 – 1959

Icky Renrut
  (Ike plays guitar)
  In Your Eyes Baby / Jack Rabbit
  Stevens 104
  1959

Little Cooper & The Drifters
  (Ike plays guitar)
  Evening Train / Moving Slow
  Stevens 105
  1959

Bobby Foster
  (Ike plays piano and guitar)
  Angel Of Love / Star Above
  Stevens 106
  1959

Icky Renrut
  (Ike plays guitar)
  Ho… Ho / Hey… Hey
  Stevens 107
  1959

Ike Turner & The Kings Of Rhythm
  (Ike plays guitar and sings A- side)
  My Love / That's All I Need
  Sue 722
  1959

Ike & Tina Turner
  A Fool In Love / The Way You Love Me
  Sue 730
  1960

Ike & Tina Turner
  You're My Baby / A Fool Too Long
  Sue 734
  1960

Ike & Tina Turner
  I Idolize You / Letter From Tina
  Sue 735
  1960

Jackie Brenston with Ike Turner & His Kings Of Rhythm
  (Ike plays guitar)
  Trouble Up The Road / You Ain't The One
  Sue 736
  1960

Ike & Tina Turner
  I'm Jealous / You're My Baby
  Sue 740
  1960

Eloise Hester (with Ike Turner)
  My Man Rock Head / I Need You
  Sue 742
  1960

Jimmy & Jean With Ike Turner's Orchestra
I Wanta Marry You / I Can't Believe
Sue 743
1960

Ike & Tina Turner
(Ike plays piano only)
It's Gonna Work Out Fine/Won't You Forgive Me
Sue 749
1961

Ike & Tina Turner
Poor Fool / Can You Blame Me
Sue 753
1961

Ike Turner & His Orchestra
The Big Question / She Made My Blood Run
Cold / Rock-A-Bucket
King 5553
1961

Billy Gayles
(Ike plays piano)
I'm Hurting / I'm Dreaming Of You
Shock 200
1961

Mickey & Sylvia
(Ike plays piano)
Baby You're So Fine / Love Drops
Willow 23000 – 1961

Albert King
(Ike plays piano on A-side)
Don't Throw Your Love On Me So Strong / This
Morning
Bobbin 131/ King 5575
1961

Dolores Johnson With Ike Turner's Band
Give Me Your Love / Gotta Find My Baby
Bobbin 132
1962

Bobby Bland with Ike Turner
Love You Baby / Drifting
Kent 398
1962

Robbie Montgomery With The Ikettes
Crazy In Love / Pee-Wee
Teena 1701
1962

Tina Turner With The Ikettes
Prisoner In Love (No Bail In This Jail) / Those
Words
Teena 1702
1962

Ike & Tina Turner
Tra La La La La / Puppy Love
Sue 757
1962

Ike & Tina Turner
Prancing / It's Gonna Work Out Fine
Sue 760
1962

Ike & Tina Turner
You Shoulda Treated Me Right / Sleepless
Sue 765
1962

Ike & Tina Turner
The Argument / Mind In A Whirl
Sue 772
1962

Ike & Tina Turner
Please Don't Hurt Me / Worried And Hurtin'
Inside
Sue 774
1962

Jimmy Thomas (with Ike Turner)
You Can Go / Hurry And Come Home
Sue 778
1962

The Ikettes
I'm Blue (The Gong-Gong Song) / Find My Baby
Atco 6212
1962

The Ikettes
Troubles On My Mind / Come On And Truck
Atco 6223
1962

The Ikettes
Heavenly Love / Zizzy Zee Zum Zum
Atco 6232
1962

The Ikettes
I Do Love You / I Had A Dream The Other
Night
Atco 6243
1962

Ike & Tina Turner
Tina's Dilemma / I Idolize You
Sue 768
1963

**Vernon Guy With Ike Turner's Band & The
Ikettes**
You've Got Me / They Ain't Lovin' Ya
Teena 1703
1963

Ike & Tina Turner
Don't Play Me Cheap / Wake Up
Sue 784
1963

Ike & Tina Turner
If I Can't Be First / I'm Going Back Home
Sonja 2001
1963

Jimmy Thomas With The Ike & Tina Turner Revue
You've Tasted Another's Lips / I Love Nobody
But You
Sonja 2004
1963

Jimmy Thomas
The Darkest Hour / The Little Cheater
Sputnik 10001
196?

Ike & Tina Turner
You Can't Miss Nothing That You Never Had /
God Gave Me You
Sonja 2005
1963

Fontella Bass –
Poor Little Fool / This Would Make Me Happy
Sonja 2006/Vesuvius 1002
1963

Vernon Guy (with Ike Turner)
Anything To Make It With You / Anything To
Make It With You
Sonja 2007 – 1963

Little Bones (The World's Greatest Singing Cricket)
(Ike sings)
What'd I Say / Ya-Ya
Prann 5001
1963

The Turnabouts
(Ike plays guitar)
Gettin' Away / Cotton Pickin'
Prann 5002
1963

Little Bones (The World's Greatest Singing Cricket)
(Ike sings)
Going To The River / I Know
Prann 5006
1963

The Nasty Minds
(Featuring Ike Turner)
Getting Nasty / Nutting Up
Sonja 5001
1963

Bobby John
(Featuring Ike Turner)
Lonely Soldier / The Bad Man
Sony 111
1963

Venetta Fields With Ike Turner's Band
You're Still My Baby / I'm Leaving You
Sony 112
1963

Stacy Johnson
(Featuring Ike Turner)
Don't Believe 'Em / Remove My Doubts
Sony 113
1963

Ike & Tina Turner Revue With The Ikettes
Here's Your Heart / Here's Your Heart (instr.)
Innis 3000
1964

Gloria Garcia With The Ike & Tina Revue
No Puedes Extranar / Koonkie Cookie
Innis 3001
1964

Ike & Dee Dee Johnson
You Can't Have Your Cake (And Eat It Too) /
The Drag
Innis 3002
1964

Ike & Tina Turner
A Fool For You / No Tears To Cry
Warner Bros. 5433
1964

Ike & Tina Turner
It's All Over / Finger Poppin'
Warner Bros. 5461
1964

Ike & Tina Turner
Ooh-Poo-Pah-Doo / Merry Christmas Baby
Warner Bros. 5493
1964

Ike & Tina Turner
I Can't Believe What You Say (For Seeing What
You Do) / My Baby Now
Kent 402
1964

Ike & Tina Turner
Am I A Fool In Love / Please, Please, Please
Kent 409
1964

Stacy Johnson With Ike Turner's Band
(Ike plays guitar)
Don't Blame Him / Consider Yourself
Modern 1001
1964

Ike Turner And His Orchestra
I'm On Your Trail / I Know You Don't Love Me
Royal American 105
1965

The Ikettes
Camel Walk / Nobody Loves Me
Modern 1003
1965

The Ikettes
Peaches 'N' Cream / The Biggest Players
Modern 1005
1965

Ike & Tina Turner
Goodbye, So Long / Hurt Is All You Gave Me
Modern 1007
1965

The Ikettes
How Come / Fine Fine Fine
Modern 1008
1965

The Ikettes
I'm So Thankful / Don't Feel Sorry For Me
Modern 1011
1965

Ike & Tina Turner
I Don't Need / Gonna Have Fun
Modern 1012
1965

The Ikettes
Sally Go 'Round The Roses / Lonely For You

Modern 1015
1965

The Ikettes
What 'Cha Gonna Do / Down, Down
Phi-Dan 5009
1965

Ike & Tina Turner
I'm Thru With Love / Tell Her I'm Not Home
Loma 2011
1965

Ike & Tina Turner
Somebody Needs You / (I'll Do Anything) Just
To Be With You
Loma 2015
1965

Ike & Tina Turner
Chicken Shack / He's The One
Kent 418
1965

Ike & Tina Turner
Two Is A Couple / Tin Top House
Sue 135
1965

Ike Turner & His Kings Of Rhythm
The New Breed, Pt. 1 / The New Breed, Pt. 2
Sue 138 – 1965

Ike & Tina Turner
Stagger Lee And Billy / Can't Chance A Breakup
Sue 139
1965

Ike & Tina Turner
Dear John / I Made A Promise Up Above
Sue 146
1966

Ike & Tina Turner
Flee, Flee, Fla / I Wish My Dreams Would Come
True
Kent 457
1966

Ike & Tina Turner
Beauty Is Only Skin Deep / Anything You Wasn't
Born With
Tangerine 963
1966

Ike & Tina Turner
Dust My Broom / I'm Hooked
Tangerine 967
1966

Ike & Tina Turner
A Man Is A Man Is A Man / Two To Tango
Philles 134
1966

The Ikettes
Da Doo Ron Ron / Not That I Recall   (B-side
written by Ike)
Modern 1024
1966

Dee Clark
I Don't Need (Nobody Like You) / Hot Potatoe
(both sides written & arranged by Ike)
Constellation 165
1966

Ike & Tina Turner
I'll Never Need More Than This / The Cash Box
Blues(Oops We Printed The Wrong Story Again)
Philles 135
1967

Ike & Tina Turner
(Ike plays piano or guitar on B-side)
A Love Like Yours (Don't Come Knocking Every
Day) / I Idolize You
Philles 136
1967

Ike & Tina Turner
Get It-Get It / You Weren't Ready (For My Love)
Cenco 112
1967

The Mirettes
In The Midnight Hour / ?

Revue 11004
1968

Ike & Tina Turner
So Fine / So Blue Over You
Innis 6667
1968

Ike & Tina Turner
I Better Get Ta' Steppin / Poor Sam
Innis 6668
1968

Ike & Tina Turner
It Sho' Ain't Me / We Need An Understanding
Pompeii 66675
1968

Ike & Tina Turner with Ike Turner and His Kings Of Rhythm
Too Hot To Hold / You Got What You Wanted
Pompeii 66682
1968

The Ikettes
Beauty Is Just Skin Deep / Make Them Wait
Pompeii 66683
1968

Ike & Tina Turner
Shake A Tail Feather / Cussin', Cryin' And Carryin' On

Pompeii 66700
1969

Ike Turner & The Soul Seven
Everythings Everything (Part 1) / Everythings
Everything (Part 2)
Pompeii 7001
1969

Ike & Tina Turner
Betcha Can't Kiss Me (Just One Time) / Cussin',
Cryin' And Carryin' On
Pompeii 7003
1969

Ike & Tina Turner
I've Been Loving You Too Long / Grumbling
Blue Thumb 101
1969

Ike & Tina Turner
The Hunter / Crazy 'Bout You Baby
Blue Thumb 102
1969

Earl Hooker – Ike plays piano
Boogie, Don't Blot / Funky Blues
Blue Thumb 103
1969

Ike & Tina Turner
Bold Soul Sister / I Know

Blue Thumb 104
1969

Ike & Tina Turner
I'm Gonna Do All I Can (To Do Right By My
Man) / You've Got Too Many Ties That Bind
Minit 32060
1969

Ike & Tina Turner
I Wish It Would Rain / With A Little Help From
My Friends
Minit 32068
1969

Ike & Tina Turner
I Wanna Jump / Treating Us Funky
Minit 32077
1969

Ike & Tina Turner
(Ike plays guitar or piano on B-side)
River Deep – Mountain High / I'll Keep You
Happy
A&M 1118
1969

Ike & Tina Turner with the Ikettes
Come Together / Honky Tonk Women
Minit 32087
1970

Ike & Tina Turner
Please, Please, Please (pt.1) / Please, Please,
Please (pt.2)
Kent 4514
1970

Ike & Tina Turner With The Ikettes
I Want To Take You Higher / Contact High
Liberty 56177
1970

Ike Turner
Takin' Back My Name / Love Is A Game
Liberty 56194
1970

Ike & Tina Turner
Workin' Together / The Way You Love Me
Liberty 56207
1970

Ike & Tina Turner
Proud Mary / Funkier Than A Mosquita's
Tweeter
Liberty 56216
1970

Ike & Tina Turner
I've Been Loving You Too Long / Crazy 'Bout
You Baby
Blue Thumb 202
1971

Ike & Tina Turner
Ooh Poo Pah Doo / I Wanna Jump
United Artists 50782
1971

Ike & Tina Turner
I'm Yours (Use Me Anyway You Wanna) / Doin'
It
United Artists 50837
1971

Ike Turner
River Deep Mountain High / Na Na
United Artists 50865
1971

The Ikettes
Got What It Takes / If You Take A Close Look
United Artists 50866
1971

Ike & Tina Turner
Do Wah Ditty (Got To Get Ya) / Up In Heah
United Artists 50881
1972

Ike Turner
Right On / Tacks In My Shoes
United Artists 50900
1972

Ike Turner & The Family Vibes
Bootie Lip / Soppin' Molasses
United Artists 50901
1972

Ike & Tina Turner
Outrageous / Feel Good
United Artists 50913
1972

Ike Turner
Lawdy Miss Clawdy / Tacks In My Shoes
United Artists 50930
1972

Ike & Tina Turner
Games People Play / Pick Me Up (Take Me
Where Your Home Is)
United Artists 50939
1972

Ike & Tina Turner
Let Me Touch Your Mind / Chopper
United Artists 50955
1972

Ike Turner
Dust My Broom / You Won't Let Me Go
United Artists 51102
1973

The Ikettes
I'm Just Not Ready For Love / Two Timin',
Double Dealin'
United Artists 51103
1973

Ike & Tina Turner
A Fool In Love / I Idolize You
United Artists 0119
1973

Ike & Tina Turner
It's Gonna Work Out Fine / Poor Fool
United Artists 0120
1973

Ike & Tina Turner
I Want To Take You Higher / Come Together
United Artists 0121
1973

Ike & Tina Turner
Proud Mary / Tra La La La La
United Artists 0122
1973

Ike & Tina Turner
With A Little Help From My Friends / Early In
The Morning
United Artists 174
1973

Ike & Tina Turner
Work On Me / Born Free
United Artists 257
1973

Ike Turner
El-Burrito / Garbage Man
United Artists 278
1973

Ike & Tina Turner
Nutbush City Limits / Help Him
United Artists 298
1973

Ike & Tina Turner
Get It Out Of Your Mind / Sweet Rhode Island
Red
United Artists 409
1974

Ike Turner
Take My Hand, Precious Lord / Farther Along
United Artists 460
1974

Ike & Tina Turner
Nutbush City Limits / Ooh Poo Pah Doo
United Artists 524
1974

Ike & Tina Turner
Sexy Ida (part 1) / Sexy Ida (part 2)
United Artists 528
1974

Ike & Tina Turner
Help Me Make It Through The Night / Baby,
Get It On
United Artists 598
1975

Tina Turner – Ike plays guitar
Whole Lotta Love / Rockin' & Rollin'
United Artists 724
1975

Ike & Tina Turner
Delilah's Power / That's My Purpose
United Artists 730
1977

Ike Turner featuring Tina Turner & Home Grown Funk
Party Vibes / Shame, Shame, Shame
Fantasy D-161 (12" Promo)
1980

UK Singles featuring Ike Turner

Ike & Tina Turner
A Fool In Love / The Way You Love Me
London HLU 9226
1960

Ike & Tina Turner
It's Gonna Work Out Fine / Won't You Forgive
Me
London HLU 9451
1961

The Ikettes
I'm Blue / Find My Baby
London HLU 9508
1962

Ike & Tina Turner
It's Gonna Work Out Fine / Won't You Forgive
Me
Sue WI 306
1964

Ike & Tina Turner
The Argument / Poor Fool
Sue WI 322
1964

Ike & Tina Turner
I Can't Believe What You Say / My Baby Now
Sue WI 350 – 1964

Ike & Tina Turner
Finger Poppin' / Ooh-Poo-Pah-Doo
Warner Bros. 1B 153
1965

Ike & Tina Turner
Please Please Please / Am I A Fool In Love?
Sue WI 376
1965

The Ikettes
Peaches 'n' Cream / The Biggest Players
Stateside SS 407
1965

The Ikettes
(He's Gonna Be) Fine Fine Fine / How Come
Stateside SS 434
1965

The Ikettes
Prisoner In Love / Those Words
Sue WI 389
1965

Ike & Tina Turner
(Ike plays piano or guitar on B-side)
River Deep Mountain High / I'll Keep You
Happy
London HLU 10046
1966

The Ikettes
Whatcha Gonna Do / Down, Down
London HLU 10081
1966

Ike & Tina Turner
Tell Her I'm Not Home / I'm Thru With Love
Warner Bros. WB 5753
1966

Ike & Tina Turner
Somebody (Somewhere) Needs You / Just To Be
With You
Warner Bros. WB 5766
1966

Ike & Tina Turner
Anything I Wasn't Born With / Beauty Is Only
Skin Deep
HMV Pop 1544
1966

Ike & Tina Turner
A Love Like Ours / Hold On Baby
London HLU 10083
1966

Ike & Tina Turner
Goodbye, So Long / Hurt Is All You Gave Me
Stateside SS 551
1966

Ike & Tina Turner
I'm Hooked / Dust My Broom
HMV Pop 1583
1967

Ike & Tina Turner
(Ike plays piano or guitar on B-side)
I'll Never Need More Than This / Save The Last
Dance For Me
London HLU 10155
1967

Ike & Tina Turner
So Fine / So Blue Over You
London HLU 10189
1968

Ike & Tina Turner
We Need An Understanding / It Sho' Ain't Me
London HLU 10217
1968

Ike & Tina Turner
I'm Gonna Do All I Can (To Do Right By My
Man) / You've Got Too Many Ties That Bind
Minit MLF 11016
1969

Ike & Tina Turner
I'll Never Need More Than This / A Love Like
Yours
London HLU 10267 – 1969

Ike & Tina Turner
Crazy 'Bout You Baby / I've Been Loving You
Too Long
Liberty LBF 15233
1969

Earl Hooker
(Ike Plays piano)
Boogie, Don't Blot / Funky Blues
Blue Horizon 573166
1969

Ike & Tina Turner
Shake A Tail Feather / Cussin', Cryin' &
Carryin' On
London 5655
1969

The Ikettes
I'm So Thankful / ?
Polydor BM 56.506
1970

The Ikettes
Never More Lonely For You / ?
Polydor BM 56.516
1970

The Ikettes
I'm So Thankful / ?
Polydor BM 56.533
1970

Ike & Tina Turner
Come Together / Honky Tonk Women
Liberty LBF 15303
1970

Ike & Tina Turner
Make 'Em Wait / Everyday I Have To Cry
A&M AMS 783
1970

Ike & Tina Turner
I Want To Take You Higher / Contact High
Liberty LBF 15367
1970

Ike Turner
Love Is A Game / Takin' Back My Name
Liberty LBF 15367
1970

Ike & Tina Turner
The Hunter / Crazy 'Bout You Baby
Harvest Har 5018/Har 783
1970

Ike & Tina Turner
Proud Mary / Funkier Than A Mosquita's
Tweeter
Liberty LBF 15432
1971

Ike & Tina Turner
 (Ike plays piano or guitar on B-side)
 River Deep – Mountain High / Oh Baby
 A&M AMS 829
 1971

Ike & Tina Turner
 Crazy 'Bout You Baby / I've Been Loving You
 Too Long
 United Artists UP 35219
 1971

Ike & Tina Turner
 Ooh Poo Pah Doo / I Wanna Jump
 United Artists UP 35245
 1971

Ike & Tina Turner
 I'm Yours / Doin' It
 United Artists UP 35310
 1971

Ike & Tina Turner
 Feel Good / Outrageous
 United Artists UP 35373
 1972

Ike & Tina Turner
 Let Me Touch Your Mind / Chopper
 United Artists UP 35429
 1972

Ike & Tina Turner
Get Back / Let It Be
United Artists UP 35448
1972

Ike & Tina Turner
Born Free / Work On Me
United Artists UP 35550
1973

Ike & Tina Turner
Nutbush City Limits / Help Him
United Artists UP/UA 35582
1973

Ike & Tina Turner
Sweet Rhode Island Red / Get It Out Of Our
Mind
United Artists UP 35650
1974

Ike & Tina Turner
Sexy Ida (pt.1) / Sexy Ida (pt.2)
United Artists UP 35726
1974

Ike & Tina Turner
Baby Get It On / Baby Get It On (disco version)
United Artists UP 35766
1975

Ike & Tina Turner
Delilah's Power / That's My Purpose
United Artists UP 36028
1975

Ike Turner & Kings Of Rhythm
New Breed (pt.1) / New Breed (pt.2)
Fleetville FV-303
1975

Ike Turner Solo Albums – USA

Dance With Ike & Tina Turner's Kings Of Rhythm   (LP)

Sue LP-2003

1962

The Gulley / Twist-A-Roo / Trackdown (Twist) /
Potatoe Mash / It's Gonna Work Out Fine /
Square Dance (Steel Guitar Rag) / Doublemint /
The Rooster / Prancing / Katanga / The Groove /
Going Home

Ike Turner Rocks The Blues   (LP)

Crown CLP-5367 / CST-367

1963

Hey Miss Tina (Cubano Jump) / Stringin' Along
(Go To It) / I Miss You So / Nobody Wants Me /
The Way You Treat Me (The Way You Used To
Treat Me) / Bayou Rock (Cuban Getaway) / The
Wild One (Loosely) / All The Blues, All The
Time (Medley – Feeling Good / Love My Baby /
Please Love Me / Boogie Chillun / Dust My
Broom / Rockin' And Rolling / Hoochie Coochie
Man / Woke Up This Morning)

A Black Man's Soul   (LP)

Pompeii SD-6003 – 1969

Thinking Black / Black Beauty / Ghetto Funk /
Black's Alley / Black Angel / Getting Nasty /
Funky Mule / Philly Dog / Scotty Souling / Up
Hard / Nuttin' Up / Freedom Sound

The Family Vibes: Strange Fruit   (LP)
United Artists UAS-5560
1972
Happy But Lonely / Heep-A-Hole-Lot / Jumpin' /
Neckin' / Bootie Lip / Soppin' Molasses / Sweet /
Sixty-Nine / D.M.Z. / I-8-1-2 (I Ate One Too) /
Pardon Me

Blues Roots   (LP)
United Artists UAS-5576
1972
You're Still My Baby / Tacks In My Shoes / The
Things I Used To Do (I Don't Do No More) /
Goin' Home / Lawdy Miss Clawdy / Right On /
Think / Rockin' Blues / That's Alright / My Babe
/ Broken Hearted / If You Love Me Like You Say

The Family Vibes: (Ike Turner Presents)
Confined To Soul   (LP)
United Artists UA-LA 051-F
1973
Beauty Is In The Eye (Of The Beholder) / Two
For Three And Three For Me / El-Burrito /
Scratch / Garbage Man / The Shakes / LA Vamp /
Ballad Of All Time Blues / Journey Through
Your Feelings

Bad Dreams   (LP) United Artists
UA-LA 087-F
1973
These Dreams / That's How Much I Love You /

One Nite Stand / Don't Hold Your Breath / (You
Can Have) The City / Flockin' With You / Take
A Walk With Me / Later For You Baby / Rats / I
Love The Way You Love

Funky Mule   (LP)
DJM DJSLM 2010
1975
Ghetto Funk / Funky Mule / Poor Fool / I Idolize
You / Sad Sam / Philly Dog / You Got What You
Wanted / Scotty Souling / Make 'Em Wait / Black
Angel / Sleepless / Nuttin Up

**Ike Turner, Tina Turner & Home Grown
Funk: The Edge   (LP)**
Fantasy F-9597
1980
Shame Shame Shame / Lean On Me /
Philadelphia Freedom / Use Me / Only Women
Bleed / Party Vibes / Lum Dum / No Other
Woman / I Can't Believe / I Don't Want Nobody
– plus Ike & Tina recordings

Get Back   (LP)
Liberty LO-51156
1985
Proud Mary / I Want To Take You Higher /
Nutbush City Limits / A Fool In love / Let's
Spend The Night Together / River Deep-
Mountain High / Honky Tonk Women / Ooh
Poo Pah Doo / Baby-Get It On / Get Back

Ike Turner's Kings Of Rhythm – 1958-1959 (CD)

Paula PCD 16 / Flyright 39
1991
Matchbox (version b, takes 5-6) / (I Know) You
Don't Love Me (take 1) / You Keep On
Worrying Me (take 2) / Box Top / I'm Gonna
Forget About You / Down And Out / You've Got
To Lose / Walking Down The Aisle (take 4) /
Matchbox (version b) / Tell Me Darling / I'll
Weep No More / Keep On Lovin' Me Baby / (I
Know) You Don't Love Me (alt.) / You Keep On
Worrying Me (take 4) / I'm Gonna Forget About
You / You've Got To Lose / Walking Down The
Aisle (take 5) / Tell Me Darling / I'll Weep No
More / Matchbox (version a, take 4)

I Like Ike! – The Best Of Ike Turner   (CD)

Rhino R2 71819
1994
Jackie Brenston & His Delta Cats: Rocket 88 /
My Real Gone Rocket: Dennis Binder & His
Orchestra: I Miss You So: The Sly Fox: Hoo-
Doo Say: Willie King with the Ike Turner Band:
Peg Leg Woman: Ike Turner: I'm On Your Trail /
I Know You Don't Love Me: Ike Turner, Carlson
Oliver & Little Ann: Boxtop: Ike Turner's Kings
of Rhythm: Matchbox (version b) / Down &
Out: Icky Renrut: Ho… Ho / Hey… Hey: Ike &
Tina Turner's Kings of Rhythm:Prancing / Steel
Guitar Rag: Stacy Johnson: Consider Yourself:

Ike Turner & His Kings of Rhythm: The New
Breed, Pt 2: Ike Turner: Takin' Back My Name /
You're Still My Baby

Dance With Ike & Tina Turner's Kings Of Rhythm   (CD)

Collectables COL-CD-5759
1996
The Gulley / Twist-A-Roo / Trackdown (Twist) /
Potatoe Mash / It's Gonna Work Out Fine /
Square Dance (Steel Guitar Rag) / Doublemint /
The Rooster / Prancing / Katanga / The Groove /
Going Home

My Blues Country   (CD)

Resurgence 4117
1998
Get It, Get It / Baby, Baby Let's Get It On / Five
Long Years / I'm Blue / My Babe / A Fool In
Love / I Miss You / Sexy Ida / Sweet Black Angel
/ Get It, Get It / A Love Like Yours (Don't Come
Knocking Everyday) / Early One Morning

Without Love... I Have Nothing   (CD)

C-YA Records – 1997
Without Love / Gave You What You Wanted /
My Sweet Black Angel / My Babe / Early One
Morning / You Can't Have Your Cake (And Eat
It Too) / Five Long Years / Show Me (How To
Make Love To You) / Right On / I Don't Know
Why I Love You So / A Love Like Yours /

Rockin' Blues / Southern California Swing

The Kings Of Rhythm Featuring Ike Turner – The Sun Sessions   (CD)

Universal / Varese Sarabande 066232 – 2001
Tommy Hodge, Get It Over Baby: Johnny
O'Neal, Dead Letter Blues: Billy Emerson, Hey
Little Girl: Tommy Hodge, I'm Gonna Forget
About You Baby (Matchbox): Raymond Hill,
The Snuggle: Billy Emerson, No Teasing Around:
Bonnie Turner, Love Is A Gamble: Tommy
Hodge, You Can't Be The One For Me: Billy
Emerson, I'm Not Going Home: Johnny O'Neal,
Ugly Woman: Raymond Hill, Bourbon Street
Jump: Billy Emerson, When My Baby Quit Me
#2: Bonnie Turner, Old Brother Jack: Tommy
Hodge, How Long Will It Last: Billy Emerson, If
Loving Is Believing: Bonnie Turner & Raymond
Hill, Way Down In The Congo: Tommy Hodge,
Why Should I Keep Trying: Billy Emerson, When
My Baby Quit Me #1: Ike Turner, I'm Lonesome
Baby (alt.take): Billy Emerson, The Woodchuck

Ike Turner & The Kings Of Rhythm – Here And Now   (CD)

Ikon IKOCD 8850 – 2001
Tore Up / Baby's Got It / You Can't Winnum'
All / Ike's Theme / Catfish Blues / Gave You
What You Wanted / I Need A-Nuddin' / Swanee
River Boogie / Feelin' Low Down / Rocket 88 /
Cold Day In Hell

Ike Turner Solo Albums – UK

Ike Turner Rocks The Blues   (LP)

Ember EMB 3395 – 1968

Hey Miss Tina (Cubano Jump) / Stringin' Along (Go To It) / I Miss You So / Nobody Wants Me / The Way You Treat Me (The Way You Used To Treat Me) / Bayou Rock (Cuban Getaway) / The Wild One (Loosely) / All The Blues, All The Time (Medley – Feeling Good / Love My Baby / Please Love Me / Boogie Chillun / Dust My Broom / Rockin' And Rolling / Hoochie Coochie Man / Woke Up This Morning)

Blues Roots   (LP)

United Artists UAG 29326

1972

You're Still My Baby / Tacks In My Shoes / The Things I Used To Do (I Don't Do No More) / Goin' Home / Lawdy Miss Clawdy / Right On / Think / Rockin' Blues / That's Alright / My Babe / Broken Hearted / If You Love Me Like You Say

Bad Dreams   (LP)

United Artists UAS 29549

1973

These Dreams / That's How Much I Love You / One Nite Stand / Don't Hold Your Breath / (You Can Have) The City / Flockin' With You / Take A Walk With Me / Later For You Baby / Rats / I Love The Way You Love

The Family Vibes: (Ike Turner Presents)
Confined To Soul   (LP)

United Artists UAG 29316
1974
Beauty Is In The Eye (Of The Beholder) / Two
For Three And Three For Me / El-Burrito /
Scratch / Garbage Man / The Shakes / LA Vamp /
Ballad Of All Time Blues / Journey Through
Your Feelings

I'm Tore Up   (LP)

Red Lightnin' RL 0016
1978
Billy Gayles: Sad As A Man Can Be / If I Never
Had Known You / I'm Tore Up / Let's Call It A
Day / Take Your Fine Frame Home / Do Right
Baby / No Coming Back / Just One More Time:
Jackie Brenston: Gonna Wait For My Change /
What Can It Be: Clayton Love: The Big Question
/ She Made My Blood Run Cold / Do You Mean
It:The Sly Fox: Hoo-Doo Say / I'm Tired Of
Beggin':Tommy Hodge: (I Know) You Don't
Love Me / the Kings of Rhythm: Ike Turner
Rock-A-Bucket

Ike Turner And His Kings Of Rhythm, Vol.1
(LP)

Ace CH 22
1980
Ike Turner with Ben Burton's Orchestra:
Troubles Heartaches / You're Drivin' Me Insane:

Brother Bell: Whole Heap Of Mama / If You Feel
Froggish: Mat Cockrell: Gypsy Blues: The Fox:
The Dream Pt 1 & 2: Dennis Binder: Early Times
/ I Miss You So / You Got Me Way Down Here:
Lonnie the Cat: I Ain't Drunk (alt.) / The Road I
Travel: The Kings of Rhythm: Goodbye Baby
(Going On Down The Line): Johnny Wright:
Suffocate / The World Is Yours

Ike Turner And The Kings Of Rhythm   (LP)

Flyright FLY 578
1981
You Keep On Worrying Me (takes 1, 3-4) / I'm
Gonna Forget About You (takes 1-2) / I Know
You Don't Love Me No More (takes 4-6) / How
Long (Will It Last) / Matchbox (takes 1-4) /
You've Got To Lose (takes 1-2 / Walking Down
The Aisle (take 1) / Walking Down The Aisle
(takes 2,5)

Ike Turner & The Kings Of Rhythm – Hey Hey   (2-LP)

Red Lightnin' RL 0047
1984
Icky Renrut: Hey Hey: Tommy Hodge: Tell Me
Why: Icky Renrut: Jack Rabbit / Ho Ho: Jimmy
Thomas: In Your Eyes Baby: Bobby Foster: Star
Above: Icky Renrut: Prancin': Bobby Foster:
Angel Of Love / I Do Love You: Icky Renrut:
Hey Hey (take 1): Bobby Foster: You're The
Only One: Johnny Wright: Look At That Chick /

Gotta Have You For Myself: Bobby Foster & the
Premiers: Shirley Can't You See / I Woke Up
This Morning: Sammy Grimes Band: I Don't
Want To Lose Your Love / Bag Pipe Special:
Little Cooper & the Drifters: Moving Slow /
Evening Train:Timothy Cooper: East St. Louis
Rock / Dear Lovin' Man / Leaving Kansas City

Ike Turner And His Kings Of Rhythm, Vol.2 (LP)

Ace CHD 146
1985
Ike & Bonnie: Lookin' For My Baby / My Heart
Belongs To You: Mat Cockrell: Baby Please:
Billy Gale: I Miss You So: Little Johnny Burton:
Talkin' About Me / Walk My Way Home / One
Day / Why Did You Go Away: Billy Gale: Night
Howler / My Heart In Your Hands: Clayton
Love: Why Don't You Believe In Me / Wicked
Little Baby: Lover Boy: Love Is Scarce: J.W. "Big
Moose" Walker: JW'S Blues / Sitting And
Wondering / Can't See You Baby

Rockin' Blues   (LP)

EMI-Stateside SSL 6008
1986
Prancing / The Things I Used To Do (I Don't Do
No More) / The Gully / Think / You're Still My
Baby / Katanga / Tacks In My Shoes / Right On /
Rockin' Blues / That's Alright / Broken Hearted /
If You Love Me Like You Say (You Wouldn't

Treat Me Like You Do) / Bootie Lip / (You Can
Have) The City / Neckin' / These Dreams /
Soppin' Molasses

Talent Scout Blues   (LP)
Ace CHD 244
1988
Billy Gayles: A Woman Just Won't Do / I'm
Tired Of Being Dogged Around
: Lover Boy: Why Did You Leave Me / Nobody
Seems To Want Me: Dennis Binder: I Miss You
So / Nobody Wants Me: Mary Sue: Everybody's
Talking / Love Is A Gamble: Jimmy Thomas:
Feelin' Good / I Smell Trouble: Tina Turner: Five
Long Years: Jimmy Thomas: Mother-In-Law
Blues / Tin Pan Alley: Bobby John: Dust My
Blues: Vernon Guy: That's Alright: Ike Turner:
Twistin' The Strings

Ike Turner & The Kings Of Rhythm –
Trailblazer   (CD)
Charly CHCD 263
1991
The Kings of Rhythm: The Big Question: Billy
Gayles: Just One More Time: Jackie Brenston:
The Mistreater: Billy Gayles: No Coming Back:
The Gardenias: You Found The Time: The Kings
of Rhythm: She Made My Blood Run Cold: Billy
Gayles: I'm Tore Up: The Kings of Rhythm: Trail
Blazer / You've Changed My Love: Billy Gayles:
Let's Call It A Day: Jackie Brenston: Much Later:

The Gardenias: Miserable: The Kings of Rhythm:
Do You Mean It: Jackie Brenston: Gonna Wait
For My Chance: Billy Gayles: If I Never Had
Known You: The Kings of Rhythm: Rock-A-
Bucket: Billy Gayles: Sad As A Man Can Be:
Jackie Brenston: What Can It Be: Billy Gayles:
Do Right Baby: The Kings of Rhythm: You've
Changed My Love: The Gardenias: My Baby's
Tops: Billy Gayles: Take Your Fine Frame Home

Rhythm Rockin' Blues – Ike Turner & His Kings Of Rhythm   (CD) Ace CDCHD 553
1995

Jackie Brenston & His Delta Cats: Rocket 88:
Lover Boy: The Way You Used To Treat Me:
Dennis Binder:I Miss You So / Nobody Wants
Me: Ike Turner & His Orchestra: Loosely (aka
The Wild One): Ike Turner: All The Blues, All
The Time (medley – Feeling Good-Love My
Baby-Please Love Me-Boogie Chillen'-Dust My
Broom-Rockin' & Rollin'-Hoochie Coochie
Man-Woke Up This Morning): J.W. Walker:
Sitting And Wondering: Dennis Binder: Early
Times: Johnny Wright with Ike Turner's
Orchestra: The World Is Yours / Suffocate: Little
Johnny Burton: Talkin' About Me / Walk My
Way Home: Lonnie "The Cat": I Ain't Drunk /
The Road I Travel: Billy Gale: Night Howler /
My Heart In Your Hands: Billy Gayles: A
Woman Just Won't Do / I'm Tired Of Being
Dogged Around: Dennis Binder: You Got Me

Way Down Here: The Lover Boy: Love Is Scarce
/ Nobody Seems To Want Me

My Blues Country   (CD)
Mystic MYSCD 115
1996 – Get It, Get It / Baby, Baby Let's Get It On
/ Five Long Years / I'm Blue / My Babe / A Fool
In Love / I Miss You / Sexy Ida / Sweet Black
Angel / Get It, Get It / A Love Like Yours (Don't
Come Knocking Everyday) / Early One Morning

East St. Louis – The Stevens Sessions   (CD)
Sequel NEM CD 940 – 1997
Icky Renrut: Hey Hey: Tommy Hodge: Tell Me
Why: Icky Renrut: Jack Rabbit / Ho Ho: Jimmy
Thomas: In Your Eyes Baby: Bobby Foster: Star
Above: Icky Renrut: Prancin': Bobby Foster:
Angel Of Love / I Do Love You: Icky Renrut:
Hey Hey (take 1): Bobby Foster: You're The
Only One: Johnny Wright: Look At That Chick /
Gotta Have You For Myself: Bobby Foster & the
Premiers: Shirley Can't You See / I Woke Up
This Morning: Sammy Grimes Band: I Don't
Want To Lose Your Love / Bag Pipe Special:
Little Cooper & the Drifters: Moving Slow /
Evening Train:Timothy Cooper: East St. Louis
Rock / Dear Lovin' Man / Leaving Kansas City

Ike Turner & The Kings Of Rhythm – Trailblazer   (CD)
See For Miles 6017 – 1999

The Kings of Rhythm: The Big Question: Billy
Gayles: Just One More Time: Jackie Brenston:
The Mistreater: Billy Gayles: No Coming Back:
The Gardenias: You Found The Time: The Kings
of Rhythm: She Made My Blood Run Cold: Billy
Gayles: I'm Tore Up: The Kings of Rhythm: Trail
Blazer / You've Changed My Love: Billy Gayles:
Let's Call It A Day: Jackie Brenston: Much Later:
The Gardenias: Miserable: The Kings of Rhythm:
Do You Mean It: Jackie Brenston: Gonna Wait
For My Chance: Billy Gayles: If I Never Had
Known You: The Kings of Rhythm: Rock-A-
Bucket: Billy Gayles: Sad As A Man Can Be:
Jackie Brenston: What Can It Be: Billy Gayles:
Do Right Baby: The Kings of Rhythm: You've
Changed My Love: The Gardenias: My Baby's
Tops: Billy Gayles: Take Your Fine Frame Home

Ike Turner & His Kings Of Rhythm – Ike's Instrumentals   (CD)

Ace CDCHD 782

2000

Ho Ho / Prancin' / The New Breed (Part 1) / The
New Breed (Part 2) / Steel Guitar Rag / The
Gulley / The Groove / Twist-A-Roo / Katanga /
Trackdown Twist / Potato Mash / Doublemint /
The Rooster / Going Home / Prancing / It's
Gonna Work Out Fine / Twistin' The Strings /
Cubano Jump (aka Hey Miss Tina) / Loosely
(aka The Wild One) / Cuban Getaway (aka
Bayou Rock) / Go To It (aka Stringin' Along) /

All The Blues All The Time (medley: Feeling
Good-Love My Baby / Please Love Me-Boogie
Chillun-Dust My Broom-Rockin' And Rolling-
Hoochie Coochie Man-Woke Up This Morning)

Ike Turner & The Kings Of Rhythm – Here And Now   (CD)

Ikon CBHCD 2005
2001
Tore Up / Baby's Got It / You Can't Winnum'
All / Ike's Theme / Catfish Blues / Gave You
What You Wanted / I Need A-Nuddin' / Swanee
River Boogie / Feelin' Low Down / Rocket 88 /
Cold Day In Hell

Ike Turner And The Kings Of Rhythm – The Resurrection, Live At Montreux Jazz Festival (CD) (French)

Isabel Records IS 640202
2003
Introduction / Back To The Chicken Shack /
Baby's Got It / Sweet Black Angel / Ike's Theme /
You Can't Winnum All /
Ike's Boogie Woogie / Catfish Blues / Mercy
Mercy Mercy / Johnny B. Goode / Only Women
Bleed / Nutbush City Limit / I've Been Loving
You Too Long / Proud Mary

Ike & Tina Turner albums – USA (selected)

The Soul Of Ike & Tina Turner   (LP)
Sue LP-2001
1961
I'm Jealous / I Idolize You / If / Letter From Tina / You Can't Love Two / I Had A Notion / A Fool In Love / Sleepless / Chances Are / You Can't Blame Me / You're My Baby / The Way You Love Me

Dynamite   (LP)
Sue LP-2004
1963
You Should'a Treated Me Right / It's Gonna Work Out Fine / A Fool In Love / Poor Fool / I Idolize You / Tra La La La La / Sleepless / I'm Jealous / Won't You Forgive Me / The Way You Love Me / I Dig You / Letter From Tina

Don't Play Me Cheap   (LP)
Sue LP-2005
1963
Wake Up / I Made A Promise Up Above / Desire / Those Ways / Mamma Tell Him / Pretend / Don't Play Me Cheap / The Real Me / Forever Mine / No Amending / Love Letters / My Everything To Me

It's Gonna Work Out Fine   (LP)

Sue LP-2007
1963
Gonna Find Me A Substitute / Mojo Queen /
Kinda' Strange / Why Should I / Tinaroo / It's
Gonna Work Out Fine / I'm Gonna Cut You
Loose / Poor Fool / I'm Fallin' In Love / Foolish /
This Man's Crazy / Good Good Lovin'

The Ike & Tina Turner Revue – Live   (LP)

Kent KLP / KST / KLMP-5014
1964
Please, Please, Please / Feel So Good / The Love
Of My Man / Think / Drown In My Own Tears /
I Love The Way You Love / Your Precious Love /
All In My Mind / I Can't Believe What You Say

Ike & Tina Turner's Greatest Hits   (LP)

Sue STLP-1038
1965
A Fool In Love / Poor Fool / Tra La La / I'm
Jealous / Mojo Queen / Sleepless / I'm Jealous /
Won't You Forgive / Way You Love Me / I Dig
You / Letter From Tina

The Ike And Tina Turner Show – Live   (LP)

Warner Bros.W / WS-1579 / Loma 5112
1965
Finger Poppin' / Down In The Valley / Good
Times / You Are My Sunshine / Havin' A Good
Time / Twist And Shout / I Know (You Don't

Want Me No More) / Tight Pants / My Man,
He's A Lovin' Man / I Can't Stop Loving You /
To Tell The Truth

Live – The Ike And Tina Show, Vol 2   (LP)
Loma 5904
1966
You're No Good / It's All Over / All I Can Do Is
Cry / A Fool For You / Shake A Tail Feather /
Ooh-Poo-Pah-Doo / Keep On A Pushin' / You
Must Believe In Me / Early In The Morning

River Deep – Mountain High   (LP)
Philles PHLP-4011
1966
River Deep, Mountain High / I Idolize You / A
Love Like Yours / A Fool In Love / Make 'Em
Wait / Hold On Baby / I'll Never Need More
Than This / Save The Last Dance For Me / Oh
Baby! / Every Day I Have To Cry / Such A Fool
For You / It's Gonna Work Out Fine

Ike And Tina Turner & The Raelettes – Souled Out   (LP)
Tangerine 15611
1966

The Soul Of...   (LP)
Kent KLP-5019 / KST-519
1966
Am I A Fool In Love / Chicken Shack / If I Can't
Be First / Goodbye So Long / Hurt Is All You

Gave Me / I Don't Need / Gonna Have Fun / I
Wish My Dream Would Come True / Flee Flee
Fla / It's Crazy Baby / Something Came Over Me
/ Don't Blame It On Me

Ike & Tina Turner & The Ikettes – In Person (LP)

Minit LP-40018 / LP-24018
1966
Everyday People / Gimme Some Lovin' / Sweet
Soul Music / Son Of A Preacher Man / I Heard It
Through The Grapevine / Respect / Medley:
There Was A Time-African Boo's / Funky Street /
A Fool In Love / Medley: The Summit-All I
Could Do Was Cry-Please, Please, Please-Baby I
Love You / Goodbye, So Long

So Fine   (LP)

Pompeii SD-6000
1968
My Babe / I Better Got Ta Steppin' / Shake A
Tail Feather / We Need An Understanding /
You're So Fine / Here's Your Heart / Please Love
Me / Freedom Sound / Crazy 'Bout You Baby

River Deep – Mountain High   (LP)

A&M SP 4178
1969
River Deep, Mountain High / I Idolize You / A
Love Like Yours (Don't Come Knocking Every
Day) / A Fool In Love / Make 'Em Wait / Hold

On Baby / I've Never Need More Than This /
Save The Last Dance For Me / Oh Baby! (Things
Ain't What They Used To Be) / Every Day I Have
To Cry / Such A Fool For You / It's Gonna Work
Out Fine

Cussin', Cryin' And Carryin' On   (LP)

Pompeii SD-6004
1969
Black Angel / Getting Nasty / It Sho' Ain't Me /
A Fool In Love / Nothing You Can Do, Boy / I
Better Get Ta Steppin' / Shake A Tail Feather /
We Need An Understanding / You're So Fine /
Too Hot To Hold / I'm Fed Up / You Got What
You Wanted / Betcha Can't Kiss Me (Just One
Time) / Cussin', Cryin' And Carryin' On / Ain't
Nobody's Business / Funky Mule / Thinking
Black / Black Beauty / Ghetto Funk / Black's
Alley

Get It Together!   (LP)

Pompeii SD-6006
1969
Betcha Can't Kiss Me (Just One Time) / T'aint
Nobody's Business / Too Hot To Hold / You Got
What You Wanted / I'm Fed Up / Beauty's Just
Skin Deep / What You Got / Cussin' Cryin' And
Carryin' On / Make 'Em Wait / Funky Mule /
Freedom Sound / Poor Little Fool / So Blue Over
You

Get It, Get It   (LP)
    Cenco 104
    1969
    Get It-Get It / I Believe / I Can't Believe (What
    You Say) / My Babe / Strange / You Weren't
    Ready / That's Right / Rooster / Five Long Years
    / Things That I Used To Do

Her Man... His Woman (LP)
    Capitol SM / ST-571
    1969
    Get It-Get It / I Believe / I Can't Believe (What
    You Say) / My Babe / Strange / You Weren't
    Ready / That's Right / Rooster / Five Long Years
    / Things That I Used To Do

Festival Of Live Performances   (LP)
    Kent KST-538
    1969
    A Fool In Love / He's Mine / Stop The Wedding /
    Please Please Please / If I Can't Be First / My
    Man / You Don't Love Me No More / It's Gonna
    Work Out Fine / If I Only Had You / I Can't
    Stop Loving You / Treat Me Right

Outta Season   (LP)
    Blue Thumb BTS-5
    1969
    I've Been Loving You Too Long / Grumbling /
    Crazy 'Bout You Baby / Reconsider Baby / Mean
    Old World / Honest I Do / Three O'Clock In The

Morning / Five Long Years / Dust My Broom /
I'm A Motherless Child / Please Love Me / My
Babe / Rock Me Baby

The Hunter   (LP)
Blue Thumb BTS-11
1969
The Hunter / I Know / Bold Soul Sister / You
Don't Love Me (Yes I Know) / You Got Me
Running / I Smell Trouble / The Things I Used
To Do / Early In The Morning / You're Still My
Baby

The Fantastic Ike & Tina Turner   (LP)
Sunset SUS-5265
1969
I'm Jealous / You Can't Love Two / If / Sleepless
/ Chances Are / You Can't Blame Me / Your My
Baby / The Way You Love Me / Fool In Love /
Tell Me What's Wrong / Letter From Tina

Come Together   (LP)
Liberty LST-7637
1970
It Ain't Right (Lovin' To Be Lovin') / Too Much
Woman (For A Henpecked Man) / Unlucky
Creature / Young And Dumb / Honky Tonk
Women / Come Together / Why Can't We Be
Happy / Contact High / Keep On Walkin' (Don't
Look Back) / I Want To Take You Higher / Evil
Man / Doin' It

Working Together   (LP)

Liberty LST-7650
1971
Workin' Together / (As Long As I Can) Get You
When I Want You / Get Back / The Way You
Love Me / You Can Have It / Game Of Love /
Funkier Than A Mosquita's Tweeter / Ooh Poo
Pah Doo / Proud Mary / Goodbye, So Long / Let
It Be

What You Hear Is What You Get – Live At The Carnegie   (2-LPs)

United Artists 2 UAS-9953
1971
Introductions / Piece Of My Heart / Everyday
People / Introduction To Tina / Doin' The Tina
Turner / Sweet Soul Music / Ooh Poo Pah Doo /
Honky Tonk Women / A Love Like Yours
(Don't Come Knockin' Every Day) / Proud Mary
/ Proud Mary (encore) / I Smell Trouble / Ike's
Tune / I Want To Take You Higher / I've Been
Loving You Too Long / Respect

'Nuff Said   (LP)

United Artists UAS-5530
1971
I Love What You Do To Me / Baby (What You
Want Me To Do) / Sweet Frustrations / What
You Don't See / Nuff Said / Tell The Truth / Pick
Me Up (Take Me Where Your Home Is) /
Moving Into Hip-Style A Trip Child) / I Love

Baby / Can't You Hear Me Calling / Nuff Said
Part 2 / River Deep Mountain High

Feel Good   (LP)

United Artists UAS-5598
1972
Feel Good / Chopper / Kay Got Laid (Joe Got
Paid) / I Like It / If You Can Hully Gully (I Can
Hully Gully Too) / Black Coffee / She Came In
Through The Bathroom Window / If I Knew
Then What I Know Know / You Better Think Of
Something / Bolic

Let Me Touch Your Mind   (LP)

United Artists UAS-5660
1972
Let Me Touch Your Mind / Annie Had A Baby /
Don't Believe In Her / I Had A Notion / Popcorn
/ Early One Morning / Help Him / Up On The
Roof / Born Free / Heaven Help Us All

Ike & Tina Turner's Greatest Hits   (LP)

United Artists UAS-5667 / UA-LA 592-G
1973
Proud Mary / Come Together / Ooh Poo Pah
Doo / Nutbush City Limits / Sexy Ida (Part 2) / I
Want To Take You Higher / It's Gonna Work
Out Fine / A Fool In Love / Baby-Get It On / I've
Been Loving You Too Long

The World Of Ike & Tina Turner – Live   (2-LP)

United Artists 2 LA 064 – 1973
Theme From Shaft / I Gotcha / She Came In Through The Bathroom Window / You're Still My Baby / Don't Fight It / Annie Had A Baby / With A Little Help From My Friends / Get Back / Games People Play / Honky Tonk Women / If You Love Me Like You Say / I Can't Turn You Loose / I Wish It Would Rain / Just One More Day / Stand By Me / Dust My Broom / River Deep Mountain High / Let Me Touch Your Mind / Chopper / 1-2-3

Nutbush City Limits   (LP)

United Artists LA 180 – 1973
Nutbush City Limits / Make Me Over / Drift Away / That's My Purpose / Fancy Annie / River Deep, Mountain High / Get It Out Of Your Mind / Daily Bread / You Are My Sunshine / Club Manhattan

The Best Of…   (LP)

Blue Thumb BTS-49 – 1973
Bold Soul Sister / I've Been Loving You Too Long / The Hunter / I Know (You Don't Love Me No More) / I Am A Motherless Child / I Smell Trouble / / Crazy 'Bout You Baby / Rock Me Baby / Early In The Morning / You're Still My Baby / You Got Me Running / Dust My Broom

Tina Turner: Turns The Country On!   (LP)
United Artists UA-LA 200
1974
Bayou Song / Help Me Make It Through The
Night / Tonight I'll Be Staying Here With You /
If You Love Me / He Belongs To Me / Don't
Talk Now / Long Long Time / I'm Moving On /
There'll Always Be Music / The Love That Lights
Our Way

**The Gospel According To Ike & Tina Turner
(LP)**
United Artists UA-LA 203
1974
Farther Along / Walk With Me (I Need You
Lord To Be My Friend) / Glory Glory / Closer
Walk With Thee / What A Friend We Have In
Jesus / Amazing Grace / Take My Hand Precious
Lord / Nearer The Cross / Our Lord Will Make
A Way / When The Saints Go Marching In

Sweet Rhode Island Red   (LP) United Artists
UA-LA 312 / UAS 29316
1974
Let Me Be There / Living For The City / I Know /
Mississippi Rolling Stone / Sugar Hill / Sweet
Rhode Island Red / Ready For You Baby /
Smooth Out The Wrinkles / Doozie / Higher
Ground

Tina Turner: Acid Queen   (LP)
United Artists UA-LA 495 – 1975
Under My Thumb / Let's Spend The Night
Together / Acid Queen / I Can See For Miles /
Whole Lotta Love / Baby Get It On / Bootsie
Whitelaw / Pick Me Tonight / Rockin' & Rollin'

Delilah's Power   (LP)
United Artists UA-LA 707-G
1977
Delilah's Power / Never Been To Spain /
Unhappy Birthday / (You've Got To) Put
Something Into It / Nothing Comes To You
When You're Asleep But A Dream / Stormy
Weather (Keeps Rainin' All The Time) / Sugar,
Sugar / Too Much For One Woman / Trying To
Find My Mind / Pick Me Up (Take Me Where
Your Home Is) / Too Many Women / I Want
Take You Higher

Soul Sellers   (LP)
United Artists / Liberty LBR 1002
1979
Nutbush City Limits / I Want To Take You
Higher / It's Gonna Work Out Fine / Workin'
Together / Honky Tonk Women / Baby – Get It
On / Come Together / I've Been Loving You Too
Long / Sexy Ida, Pt. 2 / Proud Mary / Crazy
'Bout You Baby / Sweet Rhode Island Red / A
Fool In Love / Ooh Poo Pah Doo / I Idolize You /
Let It Be / Get Back / River Deep-Mountain High

Nice 'N' Rough (The Later Grater Hits Of...) (LP)

    Liberty LBR 2600211
    1984
    Funky Street / I Heard It Through The Grapevine / Honky Tonk Women / Baby Get It On / Working Together / I've Been Loving You Too Long / Proud Mary / Nutbush City Limits / Acid Queen / Come Together / Get Back / Sweet Rhode Island Red / I Want To Take You Higher / River Deep, Mountain High (live) / Goodbye, So Long

Greatest Hits Vol. 1   (CD)

    Wea-Atlantic 91223-2 / SAJA UBK 4019
    1990 / 92
    What You See / Woke Up This Morning / Shake / I Got My Mojo Working / De Funk / Funky Bill / The Loco-Motion / Proud Mary / Ode To Billy Joe / Slidin' / Down In The Valley / Ya Ya / Driftin'

Greatest Hits Vol. 2   (CD)

    Wea-Atlantic 91224-2 / SAJA UBK 4020
    1990 / 92
    Louie Louie / Sit And Hold Your Hand / Only Women Bleed / No More Lovin' / Ain't That A Shame / Baby Get It On / Ain't Nobody's Business / Something's Got A Hold On Me / When I Lost My Baby / It's My Own Fault / Shame Shame Shame / I Know

Greatest Hits, Vol. 3   (CD)

   Wea-Atlantic 91228-2 / SAJA UBK 4021 – 1990
   / 1992
   Feel It / Knock On Wood / Money / Lean On Me
   / Tuff Hooked Up / It's Gonna Work Out Fine /
   Get Back / Tweedle Dee / Stagger Lee / White On
   White / That's The City / Drift Away

Greatest Hits   (LP / CD)

   Atlantic / Curb D2-1B-77332 – 1991
   Proud Mary / It's Gonna Work Out Fine /
   Nutbush City Limits / A Fool In Love / I Want
   To Take You Higher / Poor Fool / Come
   Together / Stagger Lee And Billy / I'm Blue /
   River Deep, Mountain High

Proud Mary – The Best Of...   (CD)

   EMI-Capitol CDP-7-95846-2
   1991
   A Fool In Love / I Idolize You / I'm Jealous / It's
   Gonna Work Out Fine / Poor Fool / Tra La La
   La La / You Should'a Treated Me Right / Come
   Together / Honky Tonk Women / I Want To
   Take You Higher / Workin' Together / Proud
   Mary / Funkier Than A Mosquita's Tweeter /
   Ooh Poo Pah Doo / I'm Yours (Use Me Anyway
   You Wanna) / Up In Heah / River Deep,
   Mountain High / Nutbush City Limits / Sweet
   Rhode Island Red / Sexy Ida (part 1) / Sexy Ida
   (part 2) / Baby-Get It On / Acid Queen

The Best Of Ike & Tina Turner (CD)

EMI-Capitol Special Products 57362
1991
A Fool In Love / I Idolize You / It's Gonna Work
Out Fine / River Deep, Mountain High / Proud
Mary / Workin' Together / Honky Tonk Women
/ Nutbush City Limits / Sexy Ida, Pt.2 / Acid
Queen

The Great Rhythm'n'blues Sessions (CD)

Tomato CD 700712
1992
Rock Me Baby / Too Hot To Hold / Betcha
Can't Kiss Me (Just One Time) / Make 'Em Wait
/ Ain't Nobody's Business / Funky Mule / I Smell
Trouble / Crazy 'Bout You Baby / It Sho' Ain't
Me / Beauty Is Just Skin Deep / Poor Little Fool /
I'm Fed Up / You Got What You Wanted

Proud Mary And Other Hits (CD)

EMI-Capitol Music Special Markets 56681
1992
Proud Mary / I Want To Take You Higher / Sexy
Ida (part 1) / Up In Heah / Nutbush City Limits /
Honky Tonk Women / Baby-Get It On / Come
Together / Ooh Poo Pah Doo

Sexy-Seductive-Provocative (CD)

Paula PCD 9008
1993
A Fool In Love / It's Gonna Work Out Fine /

Shake A Hand / Mississippi Rollin' Stone / Living
For The City / I Know You Don't Love Me No
More / You Always Be My Baby / Rockin' &
Rollin' / Never Been To Spain / Sugar Sugar /
Trying To Find My Mind / Jesus, Jesus

Golden Classics   (CD)
Collectables Col-CD-5107
1994
It's Gonna Work Out Fine / Poor Fool / Tra La
La La La / You Can't Blame Me / This Man's
Crazy / I Idolize You / A Fool In Love / Puppy
Love / The Argument / Mind In A Whirl / You
Should've Treated Me Right / Letter From Tina /
Can't Chance A Break-Up / I Idolize You (alt.) /
I'm Jealous / Tina's Dilema / Poor Fool (alt.) /
Stagger Lee & Billy

It's Gonna Work Out Fine   (CD)
Collectables Col-CD-5137
1994
Gonna Find Me A Substitute / Mojo Queen /
Kinda' Strange / Why Should I / Tinaroo / It's
Gonna Work Out Fine / I'm Gonna Cut You
Loose / Poor Fool / I'm Fallin' In Love / Foolish /
This Man's Crazy / Good Good Lovin'

The Soul Of Ike & Tina Turner   (CD)
Collectables Col- CD-5297 – 1994
I'm Jealous / I Idolize You / If / Letter From Tina
/ You Can't Love Two / I Had A Notion / A Fool

In Love / Sleepless / Chances Are / You Can't
Blame Me / You're My Baby / The Way You
Love Me

Dynamite (CD)
  Collectables Col-CD-5298
  1994
  You Should'a Treated Me Right / It's Gonna
  Work Out Fine / A Fool In Love / Poor Fool / I
  Idolize You / Tra La La La La / Sleepless / I'm
  Jealous / Won't You Forgive Me / The Way You
  Love Me / I Dig You / Letter From Tina

Legendary Superstars, Vol.1 (CD)
  Original Sound 9323
  1994
  Proud Mary / I Want To Take You Higher / Oh
  My, My (Can You Boogie) / Philadelphia
  Freedom / Only Women Bleed / A Fool In Love /
  Ooh Poo Pah Doo / It's Gonna Work Out Fine /
  I'm Blue / Something's Got A Hold On Me /
  Shake A Hand / Paid Me Back With My Own
  Coins / Twist And Shout

Keep On Pushing (CD)
  Delta-Laserlight LL 12617 – 1995
  Honey Child I'm Over You / Something / Stormy
  Weather / Why I Sing The Blues / There's
  Nothing I Wouldn't Do / I Can't Stop Loving
  You / Ain't That A Shame / Keep On Pushin' /
  Remember Baby / Ain't Got Nobody

Rockin' And Rollin' (CD)
    Delta-Laserlight LL 12618
    1995
    I Got It Ready For You / I Had A Notion / I
    Want To Jump / I'm Gonna Cut You Loose /
    Pick Me Up / Rockin' And Rollin' / A Fool For
    You / Need Some Understanding / Ya Ya / Baby
    Get It On

Come Together (CD)
    Delta-Laserlight LL 12619
    1995
    Oh My My (Can You Boogie) / A Fool In Love /
    I Gotta Man / It's Gonna Work Out Fine / Poor
    Fool / River Deep Mountain High / Come
    Together / Good Good Lovin' / I Wanna Take
    You Higher / Never Been To Spain

Livin' For The City (CD)
    Delta-Laserlight LL 12620
    1995
    Livin' For The City / Locomotion / Philadelphia
    Freedom / Shake / Staggerlee / Twist And Shout /
    Don't Look Back / Mojo Queen / You Can't
    Blame Me / This Man's Crazy

Nutbush City Limits (CD)
    Delta-Laserlight LL 12621
    1995
    Nutbush City Limits / You'll Always Be My
    Baby / Keep On Using Me / Movin' On / Shake

Rattle And Roll / Don't Fight It (Feel It) / I Wish
It Would Rain / I Keep Still Missing You / Stand
By Me / It's All Over Now / Put On Your Tight
Pants (High Heel Sneakers)

Shake, Rattle & Roll   (5-CD Set)

Delta-Laserlight LL 15962
1995
Honey Child I'm Over You / Something / Stormy
Weather / Why I Sing The Blues / There's
Nothing I Wouldn't Do / I Can't Stop Loving
You / Ain't That A Shame / Keep On Pushing /
Remember Baby / Ain't Got Nobody / I Got It
Ready For You / I Had A Notion / I Want To
Jump / I'm Gonna Cut You Loose / Pick Me Up /
Rockin' And Rollin' / A Fool For You / Need
Some Understanding / Ya Ya / Baby Get It On /
Oh My My (Can You Boogie) / A Fool In Love /
I Gotta Man / It's Gonna Work Out Fine / Poor
Fool / River Deep Mountain High / Come
Together / Good Good Lovin' / I Wanna Take
You Higher / Never Been To Spain / Livin' For
The City / Locomotion / Philadelphia Freedom /
Shake / Staggerlee / Twist And Shout / Don't
Look Back / Mojo Queen / You Can't Blame Me
/ This Man's Crazy / Nutbush City Limits /
You'll Always Be My Baby / Keep On Using Me /
Movin' On / Shake Rattle And Roll / Don't Fight
It (Feel It) / I Wish It Would Rain / I Keep Still
Missing You / Stand By Me / It's All Over Now /
Put On Your Tight Pants (High Heel Sneakers) /

I Got It Ready For You / I Had A Notion / I
Want To Jump / I'm Gonna Cut You Loose /
Pick Me Up / Rockin' And Rollin' / A Fool For
You / Need Some Understanding / Ya Ya / Baby
Get It On / Oh My My (Can You Boogie) / A
Fool In Love / I Gotta Man / It's Gonna Work
Out Fine / Poor Fool / River Deep Mountain
High / Come Together / Good Good Lovin' / I
Wanna Take You Higher / Never Been To Spain
/ Livin' For The City / Locomotion / Philadelphia
Freedom / Shake / Staggerlee / Twist And Shout /
Don't Look Back / Mojo Queen / You Can't
Blame Me / This Man's Crazy / Nutbush City
Limits / You'll Always Be My Baby / Keep On
Using Me / Movin' On / Shake Rattle And Roll /
Don't Fight It (Feel It) / I Wish It Would Rain / I
Keep Still Missing You / Stand By Me / It's All
Over Now / Put On Your Tight Pants (High Heel
Sneakers)

Fool In Love   (CD)
King 1439 – 1995
A Fool In Love / I'm Fed Up / It Sho' Ain't Me /
Too Hot To Hold / So Fine / Shake A Tail
Feather / We Need An Understanding / I Better
Get Ta Steppin' / Ain't Nobody's Business / It's
Gonna Work Out Fine

18 Classic Tracks   (CD)
EMI 52966 / EMI CDGOLD 1049 – 1996
Proud Mary / Nutbush City Limits / Get Back /

Honky Tonk Women / Living For The City / I
Want To Take You Higher / Come Together /
Higher Ground / Workin' Together / Sexy Ida / I
Idolize You / Drift Away / Sweet Rhode Island
Red / Early One Morning / I'm Yours / Love Like
Yours / I Heard It Through The Grapevine (live)
/ I've Been Loving You Too Long

What You Hear Is What You Get – Live At Carnegie Hall   (CD)

EMI 8-38309 2
1996
Introductions by DJ Frankie Crocker and MC
Eddie Burkes / the Ikettes: Piece Of My Heart /
the Ikettes: Everyday People / Introduction To
Tina By MC Eddie Burkes / Doin' The Tina
Turner / Sweet Soul Music / Ooh Poo Pah Doo /
Honky Tonk Women / A Love Like Yours
(Don't Come Knockin' Every Day) / Proud Mary
/ Proud Mary (encore) / I Smell Trouble / Ike's
Tune / I Want To Take You Higher / I've Been
Loving You Too Long / Respect

Don't Play Me Cheap   (CD)

Collectables Col-CD-5763
1997
Wake Up / I Made A Promise Up Above / Desire
/ Those Ways / Mamma Tell Him / Pretend /
Don't Play Me Cheap / The Real Me / Forever
Mine / No Amending / Love Letters / My
Everything To Me

Back In The Day   (CD)
32 Records 32013 – 1997
Don't Fight It-Knock On Wood / Humpty
Dumpty / Sugar, Sugar / Sweet Rhode Island Red
/ Stormy Weather / You Took A Trip / I Can't
Believe What You Say / Mississippi Rolling Stone
/ I Want To Take You Higher / Shame Shame
Shame / Golden Empire / Use Me / Nudden / All
I Could Do Was Cry / Rockin' And Rollin'

**Bold Soul Sister – The Best Of Blue Thumb
Recordings   (CD)**
Universal / Hip-O Hip 40051 – 1997
Bold Soul Sister / I've Been Loving You Too
Long / 3 O'Clock In The Morning Blues / You
Don't Love Me (Yes I Know) / I Smell Trouble /
Please Love Me / Mean Old World / Dust My
Broom / Early In The Morning / Crazy 'Bout
You Baby / Reconsider Baby / Rock Me Baby /
Five Long Years / I Am A Motherless Child /
Honest I Do / The Hunter

Love In Vain   (CD)
Beacon / Boomerang 51605
1998
It's Gonna Work Out Fine / Crazy 'Bout You
Baby / Somebody (Somewhere) Needs You / You
Got What You Wanted / I Smell Trouble / Rock
Me Baby / Nutbush City Limits / Living For The
City / Betcha Can't Kiss Me (Just One Time) /
Sugar, Sugar

Absolutely The Best   (CD)

Varese 1025
1998
Nutbush City Limits / I Idolize You / Come
Together / A Fool In Love / Use Me / River Deep
Mountain High / Living For The City / It's
Gonna Work Out Fine / Ooh-Poo-Pah-Doo /
Crazy About You Baby / Sugar, Sugar / I Want
To Take You Higher / Ya Ya / Knock On Wood
/ Keep On Pushin' / Never Been To Spain / Twist
And Shout / Proud Mary

Mississippi Rolling Stone   (CD)

Cleopatra / Pegasus Flight Productions CLP 0404
1998
Mississippi Rolling Stone / Living For The City /
Shake A Hand / It's All Over / Too Much For
One Woman / Rockin' And Rollin' Again / Sugar
Sugar / Crazy 'Bout You Baby / I've Been Loving
You Too Long / A Fool In Love / Cussin', Cryin'
And Carryin' On / It Sho' Ain't Me / Somebody
(Somewhere) Needs You / It's Gonna Work Out
Fine / I Can't Stop Loving You / Something's Got
A Hold On Me / Too Hot To Hold / The Hunter
/ Push / Tina's Prayer

Mississippi Rolling Stone   (CD)

Cleopatra / Pegasus Flight Productions Clp 0404
1998
Mississippi Rolling Stone / Living For The City /
Shake A Hand / It's All Over / Too Much For

One Woman / Rockin' And Rollin' Again / Sugar
Sugar / Crazy 'Bout You Baby / I've Been Loving
You Too Long / A Fool In Love / Cussin', Cryin'
And Carryin' On / It Sho' Ain't Me / Somebody
(Somewhere) Needs You / It's Gonna Work Out
Fine / I Can't Stop Loving You / Something's Got
A Hold On Me / Too Hot To Hold / The Hunter
/ Push / Tina's Prayer

Mississippi Rolling Stone   (CD)

Cleopatra / Pegasus Flight Productions Clp 0404
1998
Mississippi Rolling Stone / Living For The City /
Shake A Hand / It's All Over / Too Much For
One Woman / Rockin' And Rollin' Again / Sugar
Sugar / Crazy 'Bout You Baby / I've Been Loving
You Too Long / A Fool In Love / Cussin', Cryin'
And Carryin' On / It Sho' Ain't Me / Somebody
(Somewhere) Needs You / It's Gonna Work Out
Fine / I Can't Stop Loving You / Something's Got
A Hold On Me / Too Hot To Hold / The Hunter
/ Push / Tina's Prayer

Live And Dangerous   (CD)

Universal / Varese 1030
1999
What You See / I Want To Take You Higher / I
Wish It Would Rain / One More Day / I Can't
Stop Loving You / Ooh Poo Pah Doo / Twist
And Shout / Stand By Me / It's All Over / Proud
Mary / All I Could Do Was Cry / Suffering The

Blues / Keep On Pushin' / I Heard It Through
The Grapevine

The Ultimate Collection   (4-CD Set)
Classic World 9901
1999
I Wanna Take You Higher / Movin' On / Bootsy
White Law / River Deep, Mountain High / Keep
You Guessing / Shake / Come Together / Sweet
Rhode Island Red / Stagger Lee / Locomotion /
Philadelphia Freedom / Proud Mary / Livin' For
The City / Humpty Dumpty / Took A Trip /
Don't Look Back / Sexy Ida / I Idolize You / Ooh
Poo Pah Do / Drift Away / Golden Empire /
Shame, Shame, Shame / Mississippi Rolling Stone
/ All I Can Do Is Cry (live) / A Fool For You /
Can't Stop Loving You / Nutbush City Limits /
Do The Chicken / Stormy Weather / Feel It-
Knock On Wood / Use Me / You Paid Me Back
With Your Own Coins / Never Been To Spain /
She Can Rock / I Got It Ready For You / Why I
Sing The Blues / Early In The Morning / Rockin'
And Rollin' / Get Back / Baby Get It On / Sexy
Ida, part 1 / Hully Gully / Something / I Can't
Believe What You Say / Pick Me Up / Can't Have
Your Cake And Eat It Too / Shake, Rattle, And
Roll / Baby Take A Walk With Me / It's All Over
(live) / Keep On Pushin' (live) / You Must Believe
In Me (live) / Put On Your Tight Pants / Twist
And Shout (live)

Living For The City　(CD)

Exceed 500502
1999
Living For The City / Too Much For One
Woman / Tina's Prayer / You're Still My Baby /
If You Want It / Rockin' And Rollin' Again /
Mississippi Rolling Stone / Shake A Hand /
You're Up To Something / Raise Your Hand /
Jesus / Push / Sugar Sugar / Let's Get It On

Classic Ike & Tina Turner　(CD)

Blue Thumb 112 167-2
2000
I've Been Loving You Too Long / Three O'Clock
In The Morning Blues / Bold Soul Sister / You
Don't Love Me (Yes I Know) / Mean Old World
/ Dust My Broom / Crazy 'Bout You Baby /
Reconsider Baby / Rock Me Baby / Please Love
Me / Honest I Do / I Smell Trouble / Early In The
Morning / Five Long Years / I Am A Motherless
Child / The Hunter

Golden Legends　(CD)

Direct Source / Golden Legends GL 6152-2
2000
Rock Me Baby / Ain't Nobdy's Business / A Fool
In Love / I've Been Loving You Too Long /
Motherless Child / Bold Soul Sister / Baby What
You Want Me To Do / Reconsider Baby / I
Know / Rockin' And Rollin'

Ike & Tina Turner   (CD)
Slam 0008
2000
Living For The City / Rockin And Rollin' Again /
Sugar Sugar / Chicken / Mississippi Rolling Stone
/ Golden Empire / I'm Looking For My Mind /
Shake A Hand / Bootsie Whitelaw / Too Much
For One Women / I Know (You Don't Love Me
No More) / Never Been To Spain / Push / Raise
Your Hand

Too Hot To Hold   (CD)
Allegro / Columbia River CRG 100011
2000
Black Angel / Getting Nasty / It Sho Ain't Me / A
Fool In Love / Nothing You Can Do Boy / I
Better Get Ta' Steppin' / Shake A Tail Feather /
We Need An Understanding / You're So Fine /
Too Hot To Hold / I'm Fed Up / You Got What
You Wanted / Betcha Can't Kiss Me (Just One
Time) / Cussin', Cryin' And Carryin' On / Ain't
Nobody's Business / Funky Mule / Thinking
Black / Black Beauty / Ghetto Funk / Black's
Alley

Ike & Tina Turner Show 1965   (2-CD)
One Way 35168
2000
Finger Poppin' / Down In The Valley / Good
Times / You Are My Sunshine / Having A Good
Time / Twist And Shout / Something's Got A

Hold On Me / I Know / Tight Pants / My Man,
He's A Lovin' Man / I Can't Stop Loving You /
To Tell The Truth / Shake A Tail Feather / You
Must Believe In Me / Ooh Poo Pah Doo / Early
In The Morning / All I Could Do Was Cry /
Somebody (Somewhere) Needs You / Keep On
Pushin' / It's All Over / You're No Good / A Fool
For You

Ike And Tina Turner   (CD)

Platinum Disc 19668
2000
It's Gonna Work Out Fine / Early In The
Morning / I Idolize You / Ooh Poo Pah Doo /
Sexy Ida, Pt.1 / Workin' Together / Baby-Get It
On / A Fool In Love / I'm Gonna Do All I Can /
Come Together / Proud Mary / I Can't Believe
(What You Say) / Nutbush City Limits / I'm
Yours (Use Me Any Way You Wanna) / I Want
To Take You Higher / Poor Foo / You Shoulda
Treated Me Right / Up In Heah / Tra La La La
La / Goodbye, So Long

Shake A Tail Feather   (CD)

Music Deluxe 11
2001
It's Gonna Work Out Fine / Poor Little Fool /
Tra la La / A Fool In Love / Mind In A Whirl /
You Shoulda Treated Me Right / Stagger Lee
And Billy / Something's Got A Hold On Me /
Too Hot To Hold / Betcha Can't Kiss Me / Ain't

Nobody's Business / It Sho' Ain't Me / Mean Old
World / Three O'Clock In The Morning / Five
Long Years / Dust My Broom / Grumbling / I
Better Get To Steppin' / Shake A Tail Feather /
We Need An Understanding / You're So Fine

You Should've Treated Me Right   (CD)
EMI Music Distr. / Town Sound 90605
2002
Cussin', Cryin' And Carryin' On / Ain't
Nobody's Business / I Know / You Got Me
Runnin' / I've Been Loving You Too Long /
Shake A Hand / It Sho Ain't Me / We Need An
Understanding / Something's Got A Hold On Me
(live) / Motherless Child / Sugar Sugar / I Can't
Stop Loving You (live) / Too Hot To Hold / You
Should've Treated Me Right / Shake A Tail
Feather / A Fool For You (live) / You Got What
You Wanted / Let's Get It On / A Fool In Love

The Gospel According To Ike & Tina Turner (CD)
Varese Sarabande CD 061181
2002
Farther Along / Walk With Me (I Need You
Lord To Be My Friend) / Glory Glory / Closer
Walk With Thee / What A Friend We Have In
Jesus / Amazing Grace / Take My Hand Precious
Lord / Nearer The Cross / Our Lord Will Make
A Way / When The Saints Go Marching In

Rock Me Baby   (CD)
   Brentwood 60450 / Topline 511
   2002
   Golden Empire / Living For The City /
   Mississippi Rolling Stone / Sugar / Too Much
   Man For One Woman / I Want To Take You
   Higher / Don't Fight It-Knock On Wood /
   Stormy Weather / It Sho' Ain't Me / Tina's
   Prayer / Stagger Lee / Rock Me Baby

Portrait In Blues (3 CD Set)
   Universe UV 035 / 3
   2002
   Black Angel / Getting Nasty / A Fool In Love /
   Nothing You Can Do, Boy / Shake A Tail
   Feather / I'm Fed Up / You Got What You
   Wanted / Betcha Can't Kiss Me (Just One Time) /
   Cussin', Cryin' And Carryin' On / Ain't
   Nobody's Business / Funky Mule / Thinking
   Black / Black Beauty / Ghetto Funk / Black's
   Alley / Betcha Can't Kiss Me (Just One Time) /
   'T Ain't Nobody Business (What Me And My
   Man Do) / It Sho Ain't Me / To Hot To Hold /
   (Am I) A Fool In Love / I Better Get Ta Steppin' /
   Shake A Tail Feather / So Fine / We Need An
   Understanding / You're So Fine / Poor Little Fool
   / So Blue Over You / Make 'Em Wait / Beauty Is
   Just Skin Deep / I Can't Stop Loving You / Tell
   The Truth / Good Times / You Are My Sunshine
   / Something's Got A Hold On Me / I've Been
   Loving You Too Long / Mean Old World / 3

O'Clock In The Morning / Five Long Years /
Dust My Broom / Grumbling / I'm A Motherless
Child / Crazy 'Bout You Baby / Reconsider Baby
/ Honest I Do / Please Love Me / My Babe / Rock
Me Baby / The Hunter / You Don't Love Me /
You Got Me Running / Bold Soul Sister / I Smell
Trouble / The Things I Used To Do / Early In
The Morning / You're Still My Baby / I Know

Ike & Tina Turner albums – UK (selected)

Ike & Tina Turner's Greatest Hits   (LP)
London HAC 8247 – 1965
A Fool In Love / Poor Fool / Tra La La / I'm
Jealous / Mojo Queen / Sleepless / I'm Jealous /
Won't You Forgive / Way You Love Me / I Dig
You / Letter From Tina

The Ike And Tina Turner Show – Live   (LP)
Warner Bros. WM 8170 – 1965
Finger Poppin' / Down In The Valley / Good
Times / You Are My Sunshine / Havin' A Good
Time / Twist And Shout / I Know (You Don't
Want Me No More) / Tight Pants / My Man,
He's A Lovin' Man / I Can't Stop Loving You /
To Tell The Truth

The Ike & Tina Turner Revue – Live   (LP)
Ember EMB 3368 – 1966
Please, Please, Please / Feel So Good / The Love
Of My Man / Think / Drown In My Own Tears /
I Love The Way You Love / Your Precious Love /
All In My Mind / I Can't Believe What You Say

Finger Poppin'   (LP)
Warner Bros. WB 5753 – 1966
Finger Poppin' / Tell Her I'm Not Home /
(Please) Leave Me Alone / Just So I Can Be With
You / Too Many Tears / No Tears To Cry /

Merry Christmas Baby / Somebody (Somewhere)
Needs You / All I Could Do Was Cry / You Must
Believe (In) Me / It's All Over / A Fool For You

Live – The Ike And Tina Show, Vol 2   (LP)
Warner Bros. WB 5904
1967
You're No Good / It's All Over / All I Can Do Is
Cry / A Fool For You / Shake A Tail Feather /
Ooh-Poo-Pah-Doo / Keep On A Pushin' / You
Must Believe In Me / Early In The Morning

River Deep – Mountain High   (LP)
London HAU 8298
1966
River Deep, Mountain High / I Idolize You / A
Lóve Like Yours / A Fool In Love / Make 'Em
Wait / Hold On Baby / I'll Never Need More
Than This / Save The Last Dance For Me / Oh
Baby! / Every Day I Have To Cry / Such A Fool
For You / It's Gonna Work Out Fine

Ike & Tina Turner & The Ikettes – In Person (LP)
Minit MLS 40014
1969
Everyday People / Gimme Some Lovin' / Sweet
Soul Music / Son Of A Preacher Man / I Heard It
Through The Grapevine / Respect / Medley:
There Was A Time-African Boo's / Funky Street /
A Fool In Love / Medley: The Summit-All I

Could Do Was Cry-Please, Please, Please-Baby I
Love You / Goodbye, So Long

So Fine   (LP)

London SHU 8370
1969
My Babe / I Better Got Ta Steppin' / Shake A
Tail Feather / We Need An Understanding /
You're So Fine / Here's Your Heart / Please Love
Me / Freedom Sound / Crazy 'Bout You Baby

Outta Season   (LP)

Liberty LBS 83241
1969
I've Been Loving You Too Long / Grumbling /
Crazy 'Bout You Baby / Reconsider Baby / Mean
Old World / Honest I Do / Three O'Clock In The
Morning / Five Long Years / Dust My Broom /
I'm A Motherless Child / Please Love Me / My
Babe / Rock Me Baby

The Hunter   (LP)

Harvest SHSP 4001
1970
The Hunter / I Know / Bold Soul Sister / You
Don't Love Me (Yes I Know) / You Got Me
Running / I Smell Trouble / The Things I Used
To Do / Early In The Morning / You're Still My
Baby

Come Together   (LP)

Liberty LBS 83350 – 1970

It Ain't Right (Lovin' To Be Lovin') / Too Much
Woman (For A Henpecked Man) / Unlucky
Creature / Young And Dumb / Honky Tonk
Women / Come Together / Why Can't We Be
Happy / Contact High / Keep On Walkin' (Don't
Look Back) / I Want To Take You Higher / Evil
Man / Doin' It

Ike & Tina Turner – On Stage (LP)

Valiant VS 118

1970

Finger Poppin' / Down In The Valley / Good
Times / You Are My Sunshine / Havin' A Good
Time / Twist And Shout / I Know (You Don't
Want Me No More) / Tight Pants / My Man,
He's A Lovin' Man / I Can't Stop Loving You /
To Tell The Truth

The Fantastic Ike & Tina Turner   (LP)

Sunset SLS 50205

1971

I'm Jealous / You Can't Love Two / If / Sleepless
/ Chances Are / You Can't Blame Me / Your My
Baby / The Way You Love Me / Fool In Love /
Tell Me What's Wrong / Letter From Tina

Working Together   (LP)

Liberty LBS 83455

1971

Workin' Together / (As Long As I Can) Get You
When I Want You / Get Back / The Way You

Love Me / You Can Have It / Game Of Love /
Funkier Than A Mosquita's Tweeter / Ooh Poo
Pah Doo / Proud Mary / Goodbye, So Long / Let
It Be

Live In Paris   (2-LPs)

Liberty LBS 83468
1971

Grumbling / You Got Me Hummin' / Every Day
People / Shake A Tail Feather / Gimme Some
Loving / Sweet Soul Music / Son Of A Preacher
Man / Come Together / Proud Mary / A Love Like
Yours / I Smell Trouble / Respect / Honky Tonk
Women / I've Been Loving You Too Long / I Want
To Take You Higher / Land Of 1,000 Dances

What You Hear Is What You Get – Live At The Carnegie   (2-LPs)

United Artists UAD 60005 / 6
1971

Introductions / Piece Of My Heart / Everyday
People / Introduction To Tina / Doin' The Tina
Turner / Sweet Soul Music / Ooh Poo Pah Doo /
Honky Tonk Women / A Love Like Yours
(Don't Come Knockin' Every Day) / Proud Mary
/ Proud Mary (encore) / I Smell Trouble / Ike's
Tune / I Want To Take You Higher / I've Been
Loving You Too Long / Respect

'Nuff Said   (LP)

United Artists UAS 29256 – 1972

I Love What You Do To Me / Baby (What You
Want Me To Do) / Sweet Frustrations / What
You Don't See / Nuff Said / Tell The Truth / Pick
Me Up (Take Me Where Your Home Is) /
Moving Into Hip-Style A Trip Child) / I Love
Baby / Can't You Hear Me Calling / Nuff Said
Part 2 / River Deep Mountain High

Feel Good   (LP)
United Artists UAS 29377
1972
Feel Good / Chopper / Kay Got Laid (Joe Got
Paid) / I Like It / If You Can Hully Gully (I Can
Hully Gully Too) / Black Coffee / She Came In
Through The Bathroom Window / If I Knew
Then What I Know Know / You Better Think Of
Something / Bolic

Let Me Touch Your Mind   (LP)
United Artists UAS 29423 – 1973
Let Me Touch Your Mind / Annie Had A Baby /
Don't Believe In Her / I Had A Notion / Popcorn
/ Early One Morning / Help Him / Up On The
Roof / Born Free / Heaven Help Us All

The World Of Ike & Tina Turner – Live (2-LP)
United Artists UAD 60043 / 4 – 1973
Theme From Shaft / I Gotcha / She Came In
Through The Bathroom Window / You're Still
My Baby / Don't Fight It / Annie Had A Baby /
With A Little Help From My Friends / Get Back /

Games People Play / Honky Tonk Women / If
You Love Me Like You Say / I Can't Turn You
Loose / I Wish It Would Rain / Just One More
Day / Stand By Me / Dust My Broom / River
Deep Mountain High / Let Me Touch Your
Mind / Chopper / 1-2-3

Nutbush City Limits   (LP)

United Artists UAS 29557 – 1973
Nutbush City Limits / Make Me Over / Drift
Away / That's My Purpose / Fancy Annie / River
Deep, Mountain High / Get It Out Of Your
Mind / Daily Bread / You Are My Sunshine /
Club Manhattan

Sweet Rhode Island Red   (LP) United Artists

United Artists UAS 29681 – 1974
Let Me Be There / Living For The City / I Know /
Mississippi Rolling Stone / Sugar Hill / Sweet
Rhode Island Red / Ready For You Baby /
Smooth Out The Wrinkles / Doozie / Higher
Ground

Tina Turner: Turns The Country On!   (LP)

United Artists UA 29696 – 1974
Bayou Song / Help Me Make It Through The
Night / Tonight I'll Be Staying Here With You /
If You Love Me / He Belongs To Me / Don't
Talk Now / Long Long Time / I'm Moving On /
There'll Always Be Music / The Love That Lights
Our Way

Tina Turner: Acid Queen   (LP)
United Artists UAS 29875
1975
Under My Thumb / Let's Spend The Night
Together / Acid Queen / I Can See For Miles /
Whole Lotta Love / Baby Get It On / Bootsie
Whitelaw / Pick Me Tonight / Rockin' & Rollin'

Her Man ... His Woman   (LP)
EMI Capitol EG 26 0733 1
1976
Get It-Get It / I Believe / I Can't Believe (What
You Say) / My Babe / Strange / You Weren't
Ready / That's Right / Rooster / Five Long Years
/ Things That I Used To Do

Delilah's Power   (LP)
United Artists UAS 30040
1977
Delilah's Power / Never Been To Spain /
Unhappy Birthday / (You've Got To) Put
Something Into It / Nothing Comes To You
When You're Asleep But A Dream / Stormy
Weather (Keeps Rainin' All The Time) / Sugar,
Sugar / Too Much For One Woman / Trying To
Find My Mind / Pick Me Up (Take Me Where
Your Home Is) / Too Many Women / I Want
Take You Higher

Too Hot To Hold   (LP)
Springboard International SPB-4011 – 1982

Crazy 'Bout You Baby / Too Hot To Hold /
Please Love Me / I Smell Trouble / It Sho' Ain't
Me / Beauty Is Just Skin Deep / We Need An
Understanding / Shake A Tail Feather / Rock Me
Baby / So Fine / My Babe / Ain't Nobody's
Business / I Better Get Ta Steppin' / Betcha Can't
Kiss Me (Just One Time) / A Fool In Love /
You're So Fine

Tough Enough (LP)

Capitol / Liberty EG 2602511
1984
Stagger Lee And Billy / This Man's Crazy /
Foolish / Two Is A Couple / Prancing / Worried
And Hurtin' Inside / Dear John / You Should've
Treated Me Right / Too Many Ties (You've Got)
/ Gonna Find Me A Substitute / Sleepless /
Groove / A Fool In Love / It's Gonna Work Out
Fine / I'm Gonna Do All I Can To Do Right By
My Man / Can't Chance A Break Up

The Soul Of Ike & Tina Turner (LP)

Kent 014
1984
Goodbye So Long / If I Can't Be First / Chicken
Shack / I Don't Need / I Wish My Dreams Would
Come True / Hard Times / Flee Flee Flee / It's
Crazy Baby / Gonna Have Fun / Am I A Fool In
Love / Something Came Over Me / Hurt Is All
You Gave Me / Don't You Blame It On me / I
Can't Believe What You Say

The Ike And Tina Turner Show – Live   (LP)
Edsel ED 152
1985 / 6
Finger Poppin' / Down In The Valley / Good
Times / You Are My Sunshine / Havin' A Good
Time / Twist And Shout / I Know (You Don't
Want Me No More) / Tight Pants / My Man,
He's A Lovin' Man / I Can't Stop Loving You /
To Tell The Truth

The Dynamic Duo   (LP)
Crown GEM 004 – 1986
If I Can't Be First / Goodbye, So Long / I Don't
Need / Flee Flee Flee / It's Crazy Baby / Hard
Times / Don't You Blame It On Me / Gonna
Have Fun / I Wish My Dream Would Come True
/ Am I A Fool In Love / Something Came Over
Me / Hurt Is All You Gave Me

Collection: Ike And Tina Turner   (2-LP)
Castle Communications CCSLP 170
1987
Mississippi Rolling Stone / Living For The City /
Golden Empire / I'm Looking For My Mind /
Shake A Hand / Bootsie Whitelaw / Too Much
Man For One Woman / I Know (You Don't
Want Me No More) / Rockin' And Rollin' /
Never Been To Spain / Sugar Sugar / Push / Raise
Your Hand / Tina's Prayer / Chicken / If You
Want It / Let's Get It On / You're Up To
Something / You're Still My Baby / Jesus

Ike And Tina Sessions   (LP / CD)

Kent KEN 065 – 1987

Lose My Cool / Goodbye, So Long / You Can't
Miss Nothing / My Baby Now / Flee Flee Flee /
Makin' Plans Together / It's Crazy Baby / I Wish
My Dreams Would Come True / Something
Came Over Me / If I Can't Be First / Hurt Is All
You Gave Me / Gonna Have Fun / I Don't Need
/ Give Me Your Love / I Can't Believe What You
Say / I Need A Man / Baby Don't Do It / Over
You / He's The One / Don't You Blame It On
Me

Fingerpoppin' – The Warner Bros. Years   (LP)

Edsel ED 243 – 1988

Finger Poppin' / Tell Her I'm Not Home /
(Please) Leave Me Alone / Just So I Can Be With
You / Too Many Tears / No Tears To Cry /
Merry Christmas Baby / Somebody (Somewhere)
Needs You / All I Could Do Was Cry / You Must
Believe (In) Me / It's All Over / A Fool For You

River Deep – Mountain High   (CD)

Mobile Fidelity-MFP MFCD 10-00849
1991

River Deep, Mountain High / I Idolize You / A
Love Like Yours / A Fool In Love / Make 'Em
Wait / Hold On Baby / I'll Never Need More
Than This / Save The Last Dance For Me / Oh
Baby! / Every Day I Have To Cry / Such A Fool
For You / It's Gonna Work Out Fine

River Deep Mountain High   (CD)
EMI 869292 / Polygram Int. 393179-2
1991
River Deep, Mountain High / Sweet Rhode
Island Red / I Wanna Take You Higher /
Philadelphia Freedom / Twist And Shout (live) / I
Wish It Would Rain (live) / This Man's Crazy /
Suffering The Blues / I Can't Stop Loving You /
Tell The Truth / I Think It's Gonna Work Out
Fine / Stand By Me (live) / I Can't Believe What
You Say / Fool In Love / Good Good Lovin' /
Stagger Lee

Too Hot To Hold   (CD)
Charly CD 1042
1993
Crazy 'Bout You Baby / Too Hot To Hold /
Please Love Me / I Smell Trouble / It Sho' Ain't
Me / Beauty Is Just Skin Deep / We Need An
Understanding / Shake A Tail Feather / Rock Me
Baby / So Fine / My Babe / Ain't Nobody's
Business / I Better Get Ta Steppin' / Betcha Can't
Kiss Me (Just One Time) / A Fool In Love /
You're So Fine

**Live At Circus Krone, Munich, Germany,
November 3, 1973   (CD)**
ITM / Traditional Line Records TL-1335 1993
Intro (Family Vibes-Shaft-Eddie Burks introduces
the Ikettes) / I Got'Cha / Eddy Burks introduces
Ike & Tina Turner / She Came In Through The

Bathroom Window / Annie Had A Baby / Don't
Fight It / Get Back / Games People Play / I Can't
Turn You Loose / I Want To Take You Higher /
River Deep Mountain High / Come Together /
Proud Mary / Proud Mary (encore) / Pick Me Up
And Take Me / With A Little Help From My
Friend / Honky Tonk Women / Baby Get It On /
Respect / Nutbush City Limits (GERMAN
RELEASE)

Living For The City (CD)
Success CD 16189 – 1994
Mississippi Rolling Stone / Living For The City /
Raise Your Hand / I'm Looking For My Mind /
Shake A Hand / Bootsie Whitelaw / Too Much
Man For One Woman / I Know (You Don't Love
Me No More) / Rockin' And Rollin' Again /
Never Been To Spain / Sugar Sugar / Push /
Golden Empire / Tina's Prayer / Chicken / If You
Want It / Let's Get It On / You're Up To
Something / You're Still My Baby / Jesus

Let The Good Times Roll (CD)
Starburst CDSB 017
1995
Nothing You Can Do Boy / Cussin', Crying And
Carryin' On / Make 'Em Wait / You Got What
You Wanted / I Smell Trouble / Rock Me Baby /
So Blue Over You / Beauty Is Just Skin Deep /
Funky Mule / I'm Fed Up / I've Been Loving You
Too Long / I'm A Motherless Child / Bold Soul

Sister / The Hunter / I Know / Early In The
Morning / You're Still My Baby / You Got Me
Running / Reconsider Baby / Honest I Do / Good
Times

What You Hear Is What You Get – Live At The Carnegie   (CD)

EMI-Capitol CD 838309
1996

Introductions / Piece Of My Heart / Everyday
People / Introduction To Tina / Doin' The Tina
Turner / Sweet Soul Music / Ooh Poo Pah Doo /
Honky Tonk Women / A Love Like Yours
(Don't Come Knockin' Every Day) / Proud Mary
/ Proud Mary (encore) / I Smell Trouble / Ike's
Tune / I Want To Take You Higher / I've Been
Loving You Too Long / Respect

Sensational   (2-CD)

Charly CPCD 8257
1996

Nutbush City Limits / Golden Empire /
Something / Oh My My (Can You Boogie) /
Stormy Weather / You Don't Love Me (Yes, I
Know) / Stand By Me / Give Me A Chance / I
Idolize You / Put On Your Tight Pants / Ain't
That A Shame / Rockin' And Rollin' / Shake / I
Wish It Would Rain (live) / If You Can Hully
Gully / Betcha Can't Kiss Me (Just One Time) / I
Need A Man / I Wanna Jump / I Can't Stop
Loving You / River Deep Mountain High /

Philadelphia Freedom / You Can't Have Your
Cake And Eat It Too / Baby – Get It On / Daily
Bread / Come Together / He Belongs To Me /
Ooh Poo Pah Doo / I Want To Take You Higher
/ We Need An Understanding / Never Been To
Spain / Country Girl, City Man / Ya Ya / Why I
Sing The Blues / Living For The City / Use Me /
Sweet Rhode Island Red / The Loco-Motion /
Stagger Lee / Sugar, Sugar / I'm Movin' On

Come Together   (CD)

Hallmark 30444-2 – 1996
Oh My My (Can You Boogie) / A Fool In Love /
I Gotta Man / It's Gonna Work Out Fine / Poor
Fool / River Deep-Mountain High / Come
Together / Good Good Lovin' / I Want To Take
You Higher / Never Been To Spain

Too Hot To Hold   (CD)

Javelin / Spotlight On 127 – 1996
It's Gonna Work Out Fine / A Fool For You /
Crazy 'Bout You Baby / I Can't Stop Loving You
/ Somebody Somewhere Needs You / Too Hot
To Hold / Cussin', Cryin' And Carryin' On / I
Know / It Sho' Ain't Me / You Got What You
Wanted / Ain't Nobodys Business / Can't Kiss
Me / I Smell Trouble / It's All Over / Nothing
You Can Do Boy / All I Could Do Was Cry

The Masters   (2-CD)

Eagle EDM 016 – 1997

River Deep, Mountain High / Nutbush City
Limits / A Fool In Love / I Idolize You / It's
Gonna Work Out Fine / Poor Fool / Tra La La
La La / So Fine / Come Together / I Gotta Man /
Ooh-Poo-Pah-Dpp / Ain't Nobody's Business /
Baby Get It On / Oh My My (Can You Boogie) /
Stormy Weather / You Don't Love Me / Sweet
Rhode Island Red / I Want To Take You Higher
/ / Philadelphia Freedom / Rockin' And Rollin' / I
Need A Man / The Loco-Motion / I'm Movin'
On / Sugar Sugar / Stagger Lee / Betcha Can't
Kiss Me (Just One Time) / I Can't Stop Loving
You / Put On Your Tight Pants / We Need An
Understanding / He Belongs To Me / Never Been
To Spain / Golden Empire / Shake / Country
Girl, City Man (Take The Time) / I Wish It
Would Rain (live) / Living For The City

Ike & Tina Turner Revue – Live!!!   (CD)
Kent CDKEND 102 – 1998
Please, Please, Please / If I Can't Be First / All In
My Mind / Am I A Fool In Love / All I Could Do
Was Cry / Please, Please, Please / My Man He's
A Loving Man / I Know You Don't Love Me No
More / It's Gonna Work Out Fine / The Way
You Love Me / I Can't Stop Lovin' You / You
Should Have Treated Me Right / He's Mine /
Feelin' Good (vcl by Jimmy Thomas) / The Love
Of My Man (vcl by Venetta Fields) / Think (vcl
by Bobby John) / Drown In My Own Tears (vcl
by Stacey Johnson) / I Love The Way You Love

(vcl by Robbie Montgomery) / For Your Precious
Love (vcl by Vernon Guy)

Selection Of Ike & Tina Turner, Vol.1 (2-CD)
Golden Sounds 788
1998
I Got A Woman / River Deep Mountain High /
Come Together / Never Been To Spain /
Philadelphia Freedom / I'm Blue / Another Day /
Twist And Shout / I Can't Believe What You Say
/ Baby, Baby Get It On / Oh! My My (Can You
Boogie) / A Fool In Love / Poor Fool / I Wanna
Take You Higher / Stormy Weather / Honey
Child I'm Over You / Ain't That A Shame /
There's Nothing I Wouldn't Do / / Something / I
Idolize You / Take The Time / Why I Sing The
Blues / Stand By Me / It's Gonna Work Out Fine
/ I Can't Stop Loving You / I Wish It Would Rain
/ Keep On Pushing / Remember Baby / I Ain't
Got Nobody / I Got It Ready For You Baby / I
Had A Notion / I Wanna Jump / Pick Me Up
And Take Me Home / Rockin' And Rollin' / Ya
Ya / I Gonna Cut You Loose

Selection Of Ike & Tina Turner, Vol.2 (2-CD)
Golden Sounds 789 – 1998
Nutbush City Limits / A Fool For You Mayfield /
Need Some Understanding / Locomotion / Don't
Look Back / Mojo Queen / This Man's Crazy /
Keep On Using Me / Shake, Rattle And Roll / Put
On Your Tight Pants / I Know / Living In The

City / Shake / Stagger Lee / You Can't Blame Me
/ You'll Allways Be My Baby / Don't Fight It,
Feel It / I Keep Missing You Another Day / /
Proud Mary / It's All Over Now / If You Could
Hully Gully Stone / Sunshine Of Your Love / It's
Your Thing / Bold Soul Sister / Bootsy Whitelaw
/ Sugar, Sugar / Sweet Rhode Island Red /
Suffering The Blues / Play Your Piano / Oh Poo
Pe Doo / You Are My Sunshine / Mississippi
Rollin' Stone / Trouble On My Mind / What
Kind Of Love / Daily Bread / Fancy Annie

Let The Good Times Roll   (CD)
Pulse PLSCD 253
1998
I Can't Believe What You / Sweet Rhode Island
Red / I Idolize You / Ooh Poo Pah Do / I'm
Movin' On / I Can't Stop Loving You / You Are
My Sunshine / Early In The Morning / Tell The
Truth / Good Times / Keep On Using Me /
Golden Empire / I Gotta Man / Ain't Got
Nobody / Sugar Sugar / She Belongs To Me /
Stormy Weather / Twist & Shout

Cussin', Cryin' And Carryin' On   (CD)
Sundown-Magnum CDSB 014 – 1999
Black Angel / Getting Nasty / It Sho' Ain't Me /
A Fool In Love / Nothing You Can Do, Boy / I
Better Get Ta Steppin' / Shake A Tail Feather /
We Need An Understanding / You're So Fine /
Too Hot To Hold / I'm Fed Up / You Got What

You Wanted / Betcha Can't Kiss Me (Just One
Time) / Cussin', Cryin' And Carryin' On / Ain't
Nobody's Business / Funky Mule / Thinking
Black / Black Beauty / Ghetto Funk / Black's
Alley

Bold Soul Sister   (CD)

Prism PLATCD 211 – 2000
Bold Soul Sister / Mississippi Rolling Stone /
Living For The City / Shake A Hand / It's All
Over / Somebody (Somewhere) Needs Me / Too
Much Man For One Woman / Rockin' & Rollin'
/ Sugar Sugar / Crazy Bout You Baby / I've Been
Loving You Too Long / A Fool In Love /
Something's Got A Hold On Me / It Sho' Ain't
Me / A Fool For You / It's Gonna Work Out
Fine / I Can't Stop Loving You / Cussin' Cryin'
& Carryin' On / Push / Tina's Prayer

Ultimum Maximum   (CD)

Mystic MYSCD 143
2000
Get Back / Sweet Rhode Island Red / Crazy 'Bout
You Baby / Sexy Ida Part 1 / Sexy Ida Part 2 /
Proud Mary / I Am Yours (Use Me Anyway You
Wanna) / With A Little Help From My Friends /
Come Together / Up In Heah / Living For The
City / Nutbush City Limits / (I Want To Take
You) Higher / River Deep Mountain High /
Baby Get It On / Honky Tonk Women / Sweet
Black Angel / I've Been Loving You Too Long

The Kent Years   (CD)

Kent CDKEND 182
2000
I Can't Believe What You Say / My Baby Now /
What Do You Think I Am / Baby, Don't Do It / I
Don't Need / Goodbye, So Long / Hurt Is All
You Gave Me / Gonna Have Fun / You Can't
Miss Nothing / All I Could Do Was Cry (aka
Stop The Wedding) / I Need A Man / You Can't
Have Your Cake And Eat It Too / Lose My Cool
/ He's The One / Chicken Shack / Five Long
Years / Flee, Flee, Fla / I Wish My Dreams
Would Come True / Over You / Makin' Plans
Together / Shake It Baby / Don't You Blame It
On Me / Hard Times / Give Me Your Love / It's
Crazy Baby / Something Came Over Me

Let The Good Times Roll   (CD)

Starburst 17
2000
Nothing You Can Do Boy / Cussin', Cryin' And
Carryin' On / Make 'Em Wait / You Got What
You Wanted / I Smell Trouble / Rock Me Baby /
So Blue Over You / Beauty Is Just Skin Deep /
Funky Mule / I'm Fed Up / I've Been Loving You
Too Long / I'm A Motherless Child / Bold Soul
Sister / The Hunter / I Know / Early In The
Morning / You're Still My Baby / You Got Me
Running / Reconsider Baby / Honest I Do / Good
Times

The Very Best Of Ike & Tina Turner   (CD)

Prism PLATCD 507

2001

River Deep, Mountain High / I Idolize You /
Nutbush City Limits / Why I Sing The Blues /
Baby Take A Walk With Me / Don't Look Back /
Mississippi Rolling Stone / Come Together /
Took A Trip / I Can't Believe What You Say / I
Want To Take You Higher / Shake / Living For
The City / Get Back / Humpty Dumpty / Stagger
Lee And Billy / The Loco-Motion / Philadelphia
Freedom / Bootsie Whitelaw / Proud Mary

Funkier Than A Mosquito's Tweeter

Stateside 07243 537960 2 0

2002

Funkier Than A Mosquito's Tweeter / What You
Don't See (Is Better Yet) / I Wanna Jump / I'm
Just Not Ready For love / Young And Dumb /
The Game Of Love / Whole Lotta Love / I Love
Baby / Up On The Roof / Too Much Woman
(For A Hen Pecked Man) / Baby (What You
Want Me To Do) / (Long As I Can) Get You
When I Want You) / Bolic / Tell The Truth / The
Chopper / Wanna Take You Higher / Doin' It /
Can't You Hear Me Calling / I Like It / Popcorn /
Help Him

Also published by THE DO-NOT PRESS

A Dysfunctional Success – The Wreckless Eric Manual

'A national treasure' – Jonathan Ross
Wreckless Eric first found fame in the 1970s when he signed to the emergent Stiff Records. His label-mates included Ian Dury, Elvis Costello and Nick Lowe. Much more than a biography, A Dysfunctional Success is possibly the most entertaining read this year.

Vixen by Ken Bruen

'Ireland's version of Scotland's Ian Rankin' – *Publisher's Weekly*
BRANT IS BACK! If the Squad survives this incendiary installment, they'll do so with barely a cop left standing.

Green for Danger edited by Martin Edwards

THE OFFICIAL CWA ANTHOLOGY 2004
A brand new and delicious selection of the best modern crime writing themed on 'crime in the countryside'. The 20 contributors include: Andrea Badenoch, Robert Barnard, Carol Anne Davis, Martin Edwards, Reginald Hill, Michael Jecks, Peter Lovesey and Ruth Rendell.

Grief by John B Spencer

'*Grief* is a speed-freak's cocktail, one part Leonard and one part Ellroy, that goes right to the head.' George P Pelecanos
When disparate individuals collide, it's Grief. John B Spencer's final and greatest novel.
'Spencer writes the tightest dialogue this side of Elmore Leonard, so bring on the blood, sweat and beers!' Ian Rankin